William Howitt

Ruined Abbeys and Castles of Great Britain and Ireland

William Howitt

Ruined Abbeys and Castles of Great Britain and Ireland

ISBN/EAN: 9783744791700

Printed in Europe, USA, Canada, Australia, Japan

Cover: Foto ©ninafisch / pixelio.de

More available books at **www.hansebooks.com**

RUINED ABBEYS AND CASTLES

OF

Great Britain and Ireland.

BY

WILLIAM HOWITT.

𝔖𝔢𝔠𝔬𝔫𝔡 𝔖𝔢𝔯𝔦𝔢𝔰.

The Photographic Illustrations by
THOMPSON, SEDGFIELD, OGLE, AND HEMPHILL.

LONDON:
ALFRED W. BENNETT, 5, BISHOPSGATE WITHOUT.

1864

CONTENTS.

	PAGE.
Kenilworth Caſtle	1
Caernarvon Caſtle	28
Lindisfarne	48
Tynemouth Priory	64
Whitby Abbey	77
Netley Abbey	91
Hurſtmonceux Caſtle	99
Croyland Abbey	106
Caſtleacre Priory	122
Richmond Caſtle	130
Byland Abbey	152
Jedburgh Abbey	160
Dryburgh Abbey	174
Rock of Caſhel	188
Holy-Croſs Abbey	202
Cahir Caſtle	216

Illustrations.

Kenilworth Castle; General View	By	S. Thompson	Frontispiece
———— ; Banqueting Hall	,,	DO.	Page 9
———— ; Mervyn's Tower	,,	DO.	26
Caernarvon Castle	,,	W. R. Sedgfield	39
Lindisfarne; General View	,,	S. Thompson	49
———— ; Rainbow Arch	,,	DO.	58
———— ; Norman Porch	,,	DO.	62
Tynemouth Priory	,,	DO.	70
Whitby Abbey	,,	T. Ogle	78
Netley Abbey; Interior	,,	S. Thompson	92
———— ; South Aisle	,,	DO.	96
Hurstmonceux Castle	,,	W. R. Sedgfield	102
Croyland Abbey; Western Front	,,	DO.	109
———— ; Triangular Bridge	,,	DO.	120
Castleacre Priory; West Front	,,	DO.	123
———— ; Interior	,,	DO.	128
Richmond Castle	,,	DO.	142
Byland Abbey	,,	T. Ogle	156
Jedburgh Abbey; Western Gateway	,,	S. Thompson	172
———— ; South Porch	,,	DO.	173
Dryburgh Abbey	,,	DO.	182
Rock of Cashel; General View	,,	Dr. Hemphill	189
———— ; Round Tower	,,	DO.	194
———— ; North Transept of Cathedral	,,	DO.	201
Holy-Cross Abbey	,,	DO.	211
Cahir Castle	,,	DO.	217

Kenilworth Caſtle.

The ruined caſtle beckons me,
The abbey hoar, the foreſt dell;
By ancient halls I wander free,
And by the hermit's ſhattered cell.

HE lordly days of the old barons and the glories of feudaliſm have found hoſts of celebrators in poetry, romance, and novel literature; but in none of theſe things has any pen conferred equal intereſt with that of Sir Walter Scott. Where he has laid the ſcene of one of his ſtories, hiſtory falls into the background, and the genius of other writers ſeems to yield only a pale moonlight. Kenilworth was a great and magnificent caſtle, inhabited by princes royal, and the powerful favourites of princes: ſieges ſtout from time to time girt its walls, and gorgeous pageants enlivened its halls and courts and gardens; but had not Sir Walter Scott made it the theme of one of his moſt thrilling romances, its ivied ruins would now have ſtood little regarded, though Queen Elizabeth feaſted there, though the Earl of Leiceſter gave the

most elaborate entertainments, and Lancham described them at minutest length. It is not the glory of Elizabeth, or the greatness of Leicester, which flings a halo of beauty on the crumbling battlements of Kenilworth; but the spirit of a sweeter apparition—of one who never in reality seems to have been there at all—Amy Robsart. They who pass the dark walls of Cumnor, may shudder at the nocturnal tragedy which occurred there; but the feeling is not more real or vivid than that which haunts us at the sight of Kenilworth, innocent as it is of that horror.

Kenilworth Castle claims a high antiquity. There was a castle here, indeed, according to Dugdale, in the Saxon times, which stood on a hill called Hom, or Holme, Hill, which was battered down in the war betwixt King Edmund and Canute the Dane. This castle was situated on the bank of the Avon, in the woods opposite to Stoneleigh Park. There does not appear to have been any rebuilding of a castle on the estate so long as it remained in the hands of the crown. At the time of the Norman survey, Kenilworth was found in possession of two vassals of the king, one of whom held what was called Optone, or the higher portion, and the other the lower part. In Henry I.'s reign he granted the manor to Geoffrey de Clinton, who built a castle on the present site, as well as a monastery near it. Henry III. granted the privileges of a market on Tuesday each week, and an annual fair of three days, to the village which grew up under its protection; but these privileges died out from apparent absence of any necessity for them, till the Earl of Leicester obtained a fresh grant of them from Queen Elizabeth. Geoffrey de Clinton, who rose from a humble origin to become Lord Chief Justice under Henry I., however, did not hand down this fair possession to his family. In the reign of

Henry II. we again find it in the hands of the crown, and garrisoned by the monarch in the rebellion against him of his own son Henry, who died before him. In the reigns of John and Henry III. the castle was enlarged throughout, to meet the demands of those turbulent times. In the reign of the latter monarch, he granted it to Simon de Montfort, Earl of Leicester, and to Eleanor his wife; but only for their respective lives.

The story of Simon de Montfort is one of the most remarkable of those days. This baron, who played so conspicuous a part in the reign of Henry III., was the son of that Count de Montfort who had gained an unenviable celebrity in the persecutions of the Albigenses, in the South of France. He became Earl of Leicester in right of his mother Amicia, and, coming to England, was received in high favour by the king, and married Eleanor, the Countess Dowager of Pembroke, King Henry's sister. Much opposition was made to this great match, especially by Richard, Earl of Cornwall, and titular king of the Romans, Henry III.'s brother, and most powerful support. Simon de Montfort, however, having secured the bride, soon set himself to win the affections of the English people, and, though a foreigner, to oppose the titles of foreigners who surrounded the throne, and preyed on the country. He became the leader of the barons against the encroachments of royal power, and thus excited an enmity in the king against him, as great as had been his regard for him. He was banished the court; yet in a while, probably to remove him from the opposition in England, he was made governor of Guienne. Here the same spirit of reform, or rather of repression of the assumptions and rapacity of the nobles, aroused an outcry against him; he was recalled, and received so insolently by Henry, that the proud de Montfort told the monarch that but for his royal rank he would have made him repent of the wrong on the spot. Leicester again retired to France, but was after a time reconciled to the monarch, returned to England, and resumed the work of popular, or rather baronial, opposition. He was elected leader of the barons, who received the king in May, 1258, in Westminster Hall, armed, and demanding sweeping reforms in the government. From this time till 1267, or nine years, the contest went on in Parliament, and by arms, betwixt the barons with Leicester at their head, and the royal party, chiefly conducted by Prince Edward, afterwards the renowned Edward I. For a time Montfort was in possession of both the king and the prince; but the latter escaping, came against him, and defeated him in a great battle at Evesham, in August, 1265, and released his father, the old king. Simon de Montfort was not only killed in this battle, but barbarously mutilated. His son, also Simon de Montfort, however, continued the contest for about two years longer, and had strong forces in the isles of Ely and Axholm, the Cinque Ports, at Kenilworth, and in the forests of Hampshire. Finding it impossible to put down the baronial power, the king consented to compromise, and at Kenilworth the conflicting parties came to an agreement, which was called the Dictum de Kenilworth. The Earl of Gloucester, however, did not come in to the terms of the Dictum. He and others deemed the treatment awarded to the young de Montfort and his family too severe, and the guarantees of the Dictum too precarious. Supported by the Londoners, they stood out till November of 1267,—two years and three months after the battle of Evesham. The king then consented to a further acceptance of the concessions which had been demanded by the great Simon de Montfort, called by the people "Simon the Righteous;" and thus closed this long popular strife, excited by the poffeffor of Kenilworth. But here did not entirely end the tragic confequences.

When the pacification of the country was effected, Prince Edward, and Henry his coufin, fon of the King of the Romans, fet out for a crufade in the Holy Land. Prince Henry being in 1270 fent home on a fecret miffion by Prince Edward, took his way through Italy; and one morning being at prayers in a church at Viterbo, heard a well-known voice exclaim:— "Thou traitor, Henry,—thou fhalt not efcape!" Turning round, he faw, to his confternation, Simon and Guy de Montfort, who, with their mother, the Countefs of Leicefter, King Henry's own fifter, had been excepted from the conditions of the Dictum de Kenilworth; their eftates confifcated, and themfelves banifhed the realm.

Thefe embittered enemies had become aware of his prefence in Viterbo, and now appeared in complete armour and with drawn fwords making towards him. He rufhed forward and clung to the holy altar, before which he was kneeling; but in vain did the priefts endeavour to defend him. Two of them were themfelves killed by the enraged Anglo-Normans, and Prince Henry was affaffinated, and his body horribly mutilated, in revenge for the treatment of their father at Evefham. Guy de Montfort had married the daughter of Count Aldobrandini, and by his aid the murderers were enabled to make their efcape. The fhock of this news haftened the death of the King of the Romans, Prince Henry's father, and, as is fuppofed, that alfo of his uncle, Henry III., who died in November, 1272.

On the furrender of the caftle of Kenilworth, Henry III. beftowed it on Edmund, his younger fon, whom he created Earl of Leicefter and Lancafter. During the more firm fway of Edward I., Kenilworth became as gay with feftivity as it had hitherto been ftern with war. In the feventh year of that reign a grand tournament was held at the caftle. Roger Mortimer, Earl of March, was the great promoter of this feftival, and was the principal challenger of the tilt-yard. There were a hundred knights and a hundred ladies affembled, and it was regarded as a fign of the fplendour of the occafion that the ladies were attired in *filken* mantles. The dances were not lefs gallantly attended than the lifts; and, to avoid all painful diftinctions in regard to precedence, the whole party banqueted at a *round table*. Thefe exercifes began on the eve of St. Matthew, and continued till the day after the feaft of St. Michael.

On the attainder of Thomas, Earl of Lancafter, fon of Earl Edmund, the caftle again reverted to the crown, and was defigned by Edward II. as a place of retirement, when he faw dangers arifing on all fides; but it became fo to him in a very different fenfe to that which he propofed.

Edward's weaknefs and favouritifm had alienated his fubjects, and had loft him that command in Scotland which his warlike father had acquired at the coft of fo many lives, and fo much treafure. He had in that country men as brave as he was pufillanimous to contend with. Robert Bruce and Douglas defeated him at Bannockburn, and afterwards drove him from Scotland. At home, his infane attachment to the Gafcon favourite, Piers Gavefton, had difgufted the whole country, and had caufed the death of the vain foreigner at Blacklow Hill, only three miles from Kenilworth, under the hands of the Earl of Warwick, the Black Dog of Arden, and other barons. Again the Defpenfers, father and fon, engroffed his favour, and funk him for ever in the regard of his fubjects, by their unchecked affumptions and rapacity. The father was feized and hanged at Briftol; the fon, after fleeing to sea with the infatuated king, and wandering with him for weeks in disguise in the woods of South Wales, near Neath, was seized and hanged at Hereford, with some other of the wretched monarch's followers; the Earl of Arundel being beheaded on the same occasion.

Thus reduced to the lowest extremity of disgrace and misery, deserted by his wife, and in opposition to his son, the fugitive and now captive king was in the hands of Henry, Earl of Lancaster, the brother of Thomas, the earl who had been taken in insurrection at Boroughbridge, in Yorkshire, and beheaded at Pontefract by Edward's order. A more humiliating condition cannot be conceived than that of Edward here. In the castle which he had seized as the forfeited property of the attainted earl, he was now held close prisoner by that earl's brother and his own cousin; his favourites successively destroyed; his party annihilated; his wife and heir—a boy of only fourteen—alienated from him, and not a subject in the realm but anxious to be well rid of him.

After being kept at Kenilworth two months, Parliament met, declared that he had ceased to reign, and proclaimed his son, the Prince of Wales, amid universal acclamation. A bill was introduced by Stratford, Bishop of Hereford, charging Edward with incapacity, cruelty, oppression, and a number of other crimes, and ordering his deposition. This was passed without opposition; and on the 20th of January, 1327, a deputation, consisting of bishops, earls, barons, two knights from each shire, and two representatives of each borough, waited on him here, and informed him of what had taken place, and that he was no longer king. The fallen monarch received this solemn deputation in the great hall of the castle, wrapt only in a black gown, and formally renounced all right to the crown, except in favour of his son, which he thanked them for recognising. It is said that, glancing round on the individuals of the deputation, his eye no sooner fell on one than he dropped senseless to the ground. This was Adam Orleton, Bishop of Hereford, whom he had deprived of his see, and who had thence proved one of his most powerful enemies. Orleton had headed the party of the guilty Isabella, his queen, against him, and had done more to the ruin of his character with the people, by spreading the stories of his disgraceful conduct with his favourites, than any man living. Then Sir William Trussel, the speaker of the whole Parliament, pronounced the sentence of that august body; Sir Thomas Blount, the steward of the royal household, broke his white staff of office, as at the death of a king, and pronounced all persons engaged in Edward's service discharged and freed by that act. The deputation then departed, leaving the son of the powerful monarch Edward I., and the father of the equally powerful Edward III., the most helpless, isolated, and abject individual in the realms over which he had so lately ruled.

On the 24th of the same month proclamation was made in London of his deposition, and on the 29th the young king was crowned. He was by Parliament placed under the regency of his mother, the licentious Isabella, and she was herself under the absolute influence of Roger Mortimer, "the gentle Mortimer;" so that Edward in his solitary prison had the mortification of hearing that his wife, who had despised and helped to put him down, and her paramour, were actually reigning in his stead. But they did not forget him, though he now appeared so impotent: they were afraid that there might be some revulsion in his favour, especially as the clergy had the boldness to denounce from the pulpit the scandalous connection of Isabella and Mortimer. They complained that the Earl of

Lancaster favoured the deposed king too much, though Lancaster had the memory of the death of his brother to prevent too much lenity. But Lancaster was a humane and honourable man; Edward was, therefore, taken out of his hands, and put into those of Sir John Maltravers, a man of a fierce and

KENILWORTH CASTLE: BANQUETING HALL.

savage temperament, smarting under grievous wrongs from the king and his favourites. This brutal executioner removed the unhappy monarch from Kenilworth, carried him from castle to castle, heaped the most cruel indignities on him, and completed the horrible tragedy at Berkeley Castle in a manner which yet shrieks through history.

Edward III. restored the castle and estate of Kenilworth to Henry, Earl of Lancaster, for his services in placing him on the throne, and in the removal of the late king. By his marriage with Blanche, the grand-daughter of this earl, John of Gaunt, the son of Edward III., became possessed of Kenilworth, with the title of Duke of Lancaster. To him the castle owed both extension and improvement. The great Banqueting Hall is said to have been of his erection, with most of those portions of the castle called the Lancaster Buildings, forming the western side of the quadrangle. Again the castle and estate returned to the crown, through Henry IV. the son of John of Gaunt, deposing Richard II., and seizing the throne. It remained the royal property till the reign of Queen Elizabeth, who conferred it with many other estates on her favourite, Robert Dudley, Earl of Leicester. Leicester, with the ambition and display natural to him, determined to make Kenilworth one of the most princely mansions in the kingdom. He expended £60,000—equal to half a million of our present money—in restoring, enlarging, and embellishing it. He built the great entrance gateway and tower on the north side, equal itself to many baronial castles in strength and extent. He built also the part of the east front called Leicester Buildings. He is said to have refitted the great banqueting hall of John of Gaunt, and the range of buildings on the south side, between the buildings named after him and the Lancaster Buildings. He also rebuilt Mortimer's Tower and the Gallery Tower at the opposite ends of the Tilt-yard. Having completed these magnificent works, he invited his royal mistress, to whom he was indebted for this superb house and estate, to witness his lordly state there. This took place in 1566; and Elizabeth was so much pleased with the entertainment that she repeated the visit in 1568, and a third time in 1575. It is the last of these visits that has been celebrated by Sir Walter Scott in his romance of Kenilworth, and has thus conferred a greater interest upon it than it could ever have derived from the whole series of its historical events. There are some particulars of the description of the general appearance and condition of Kenilworth at this epoch, by Scott, that we may quote as making much clearer that which has to follow:—

"The outer wall of this splendid and gigantic structure enclosed seven acres, a part of which was occupied by extensive stables, and by a pleasure garden, with its trim arbours and parterres, and the rest formed the large base-court, or outer yard, of the noble castle. The lordly structure itself, which rose near the centre of this spacious enclosure, was composed of a huge pile of magnificent castellated buildings, apparently of different ages, surrounding an inner court, and bearing in the names attached to each portion of the magnificent mass, and in the armorial bearings which were there blazoned, the emblems of mighty chiefs who had long passed away, and whose history, could ambition have lent ear to it, might have read a lesson to the haughty favourite who had now acquired and was augmenting the fair domain. . . . . The external wall of this royal castle was, on the south and west sides, adorned and defended by a lake, partly artificial, across which Leicester had constructed a stately bridge, that Elizabeth might enter the castle by a path hitherto untrodden, instead of the usual entrance to the northward, over which he had erected a gate-house, or barbican, which still exists, and is equal in extent, and superior in architecture, to the baronial castle of many a northern chief. Beyond the lake lay an extensive chase, full of red deer, fallow deer, roes, and every species of game; and abounding with lofty trees, from amongst which the extended front and massive towers of the castle were seen to rise in majesty and beauty."

To give a more distinct idea of this superb place, the visitor has only to suppose himself entering by the great gateway on the north, when, advancing along the great court southward, he would find himself in front of the eastern façade. The great massive tower at his right hand is Cæsar's Tower, supposed to be so called from a resemblance to the Tower of London, but evidently Norman, and no doubt built by Geoffrey de Clinton. At his left hand, and forming the south-eastern angle, stands Leicester's more modern and ornate Tower, with its large Elizabethan windows; and between them runs a lower range, called King Henry VIII.'s Lodgings and Sir Robert Dudley's Lobby. Betwixt Dudley's Lobby, King Henry's Lodgings, and Cæsar's Tower, is the arched main entrance to the interior court of the castle. At the opposite side of the quadrangle rises Lancaster's great banqueting hall, facing westward over the lake; and at its north-west angle rises Mervyn's or the Strong Tower, where Scott imagines Amy Robsart to have taken up her quarters, on her recent visit to the castle, during the great festival. The buildings betwixt Lancaster's Buildings and Leicester's, face the lake southward.

The spectator, whilst making these observations, would have behind him the two towers, called Lun's Tower and the Water Tower, built in the battlemented court wall, and with the moat outside. To his left hand he would have the Gallery Tower and Mortimer's Tower, with the Tilt-yard between them, and the lake coming up to them. Beyond them and the lake would spread the chase; and on the right hand of the castle he would see the garden extending, with its statues and broad walks, to the Pleasaunce and the Swan Tower, both washed by the lake on the west. Such was the aspect of the place at the moment of the arrival of Queen Elizabeth. Of that arrival and vifit we have the quaint, conceited, but graphic defcription of Mafter Robert Laneham, " Clerk of the Council-Chamber door, and alfo Keeper of the fame." Scott calls Laneham " as great a coxcomb as ever blotted paper ;" and no doubt he deferves the epithet: neverthelefs, he has left us a very amufing account of this remarkable vifit, in very antiquated language. He ftyles it " A Letter, whearin, part of the Entertainment, untoo the Queenz Maiefty, at Killingworth Caftle, in Warwick Sheer, in this Soomers Progrefs, 1575, iz fignified: from a freend Officer attendant in the Coourt, unto hiz freend, a Citizen and Merchaunt of London."

Before introducing fome touches from Laneham's account, it is worth while taking a note or two of himfelf. Robert Laneham was a Nottinghamfhire man, who had travelled as a merchant-adventurer in fundry countries, and had picked up enough knowledge of French, Dutch, and Spanifh, to enable him to converfe with perfons from thofe countries on ordinary topics. Befides this, he could play on the guitar, citern and virginals; had been a gallant amongft the ladies, and a *bon vivant* amongft the men. He was fond of fack and fugar, which he fays made him " flufh fo mooch a dayz ;" that is, have a very florid face. He was juft the man to fuit the Earl of Leicefter, and by him was introduced to this poft at court, and, as Laneham boafts, did him many favours befides ; gave him apparel from his own back, got him allowance on the ftable, and helped him in his licence of beans, one of thofe endlefs monopolies which oppreffed the country under Elizabeth. In confequence, fays Laneham, " I now go in my filks, that elfe might ruffle in my cut-canvas; ride on horfeback, that elfe might manage on foot; am known to their honours, and taken forth with the beft, that elfe might be bid to ftand back." How he exercifed his office, he thus tells us :—"When the Council fit I am at hand. If any make a babbling,—'Peace!' I fay. If I take liftener or a prier in at the chincks or lock-hole, I am bye and bye at the bones of him. If a friend come, I make him fit down by me on a form or cheft—let the reft walk a God's name!" He adds, "And here do my languages now and then ftand me in good ftead: my French, my Spanifh, my Dutch, and my Latin. Sometimes amongft the ambaffadors' men, if their mafter be within council; fometimes with the ambaffador himfelf, if he defire me to call for his fervant, or afk me what it is o'clock; and I warrant you I anfwer him fo boldly, that they wonder to fee fuch a fellow there."

We may from thefe paffages fee exactly Laneham's vanity and felf-confidence. He was by no means backward at putting himfelf amongft his fuperiors; and no doubt, his language, his mufic, and his airs of foreign travel, made him amufing to them. Accordingly, he tells us that during the queen's feventeen days' ftay at Kenilworth, he fpent many afternoons and evenings with Sir George Howard, and fometimes at Lady Sidney's chambers, "but always amongft the gentlewomen, by my good-will."

It was the rule at that day, as we find from a very rare book of 1671, that courtiers waiting in the ante-chamber or prefence-chamber were not to walk up and down, not to whiftle or fing for divertifement: if any one did fo, it was the ufher's duty to rebuke him. What was more curious, "it was uncivil to knock hard, or give more than one knock." "To knock is no lefs than brutifh; the way is to fcratch with the nails." "If nobody was in the ante-chamber to introduce you, you muft try gently if the door be locked or bolted infide. If it were, you muft not knock or fiddle about the lock like an impatient perfon, as if he would pick it; but you muft patiently wait till it is opened, or fcratch foftly to make them hear; but if nobody comes, you muft retire to fome diftance, left you fhould be fufpected of eaves-dropping, which would be a great offence to all perfons of quality." It was confidered but civil for a perfon thus waiting to walk with his hat off in halls and ante-chambers. Thefe were the rules that Laneham had to enforce.

Laneham opens his narrative of the queen's vifit with her arrival at Long Ichington, "a town and lordfhip of my lord's" within feven miles of Kenilworth, where Leicefter gave " her majefty a great cheer, dinner, and pleazaunt paftime in hunting by the way after, that it was eight in the evening ear her highnefs came too Killingworth." Laneham always calls it Killingworth; though he fays it was originally Kenelworth, fo named from Kenelm, or Kenulph, the firft builder of the caftle. Killingworth was the name commonly ufed at the time.

The whole of the ceremonies of the queen's reception and entertainment during her ftay were laid down in a mafque compofed by George Gafcoigne, the poet, ftyled " The Princely Pleafures at the Courte at Kenelworth; that is to faye, the copies of all fuch Verfes, Profes, or poetical inventions, and other Deuices of Pleafure, as were there deuifed by fundry gentlemen before the Queen's Majeftie, in the year 1575." This, with all its long and adulatory addreffes in verfe and profe, which met Elizabeth at every turn from the mouths of all forts of heathen deities, may be found, as well as Laneham's narrative, in the firft volume of Nicol's " Progreffes of Queen Elizabeth." Sir Walter Scott has fo fully defcribed them in his romance, that we may be excufed taking more than a paffing notice of them.

As the queen approached the firft gate, a perfon clad to reprefent one of the Sibyls accofted her with a poem; at the next gate of the bridge or tilt-yard, a gigantic porter with huge club and keys made another addrefs, and the trumpeters on the gate founded their trumpets in welcome. Then a perfon attired as the famous Lady of the Lake of King Arthur's ftory, came on a floating ifland to do homage at the fecond gate. On the different pairs of pofts of the continuation of the bridge over a dry valley from the tilt-yard to the caftle-gate between which the queen paffed, were placed cages with birds, green ears of corn as the gifts of Ceres, different kinds of fruits, oranges, lemons, pomegranates, &c.; grapes, wine, in livery pots of filver; another pair of pofts had a great difplay of fifh; another a collection of arms and armour; another of mufical inftruments. Over the entrance gate itfelf were fufpended her majefty's arms, and a Latin poem in her honour; every letter mentioning her majefty being in gold. Thefe verfes were recited by a poet crowned with bay, and in a long cerulean garment. In the caftle the queen was received with feafting, dancing, and a vifit from Jupiter Tonans himfelf, amidft burning darts, lightnings, and thunders. During the feventeen days that the entertainment lafted, Elizabeth could not turn any way, but pagan gods and goddeffes, favage men, fylvans, and nymphs, befet her path. Sometimes fhe hunted in the park, whence invifible beings fpoke out of trees and thickets; fometimes fhe enjoyed one of her moft favourite delights, a bear-baiting; and Laneham luxuriates in the defcription of this favage fport, where thirteen bears at once were attacked by the dogs; and he details with the greateft gufto how the ban-dogs tore the bears by the throat, and clawed them by the fcalp, "with roring, toffing, tumbling; how the bear would work to wynd himfelf from them; and when he was lofe, to fhake his ears twyfe or thryfe with the blood and flaver about fizaling, wos a matter of good relief."

One day they had the famous Coventry Hoketide play under the management of a Captain Cox, " an old man I promiz yoo," fo famous for this reprefentation that Ben Jonfon wrote a " Mafque of Owls at Kenilworth " to introduce him on his hobby-horfe. At other times they had all forts of feats of agility difplayed by an Italian, and at night again fireworks. They had all kinds of country fports,—the quintain, running, wreftling, even a country wedding celebrated. Amongft other characters, a minftrel appeared in full coftume, and recited paffages from the Acts of King Arthur; and Laneham runs into a great eulogy on bone fpoons as they appeared ftanding upright in a bowl of furmenty in the minftrel's creft; " how, beeing nether fo churlifh in weight az is metal, nor fo froward and brittle to manure (manufacture) az ftone; nor yet fo foily in ufe nor roough to the lips az wood is; but lyght, plyaunt, und fmooth; thot with a little licking, wool allweiz be kept as clean as a dy."

The manners of the time were not very refined. On the next page he tells us that the minftrel, preparing himfelf to recite, " cleered his vois with a hem and a reach, and fpat oout withal; wyped his lips with the hollo of his hand (for fyling his napkin), tempered a ftring or too with his wreaft, and after a little warbling on his harp for a prelude, began."

The flattery fhowered on the queen was without any ftint; often as coarfe as the manners, and fometimes abfolutely blafphemous. The fcene of the Echo, afterwards fo happily burlefqued by Butler in his Hudibras, is enacted between a favage man all in ivy, and the faid Echo, in which the adulation is ftupendous, and yet not a whit beyond the capacious fwallow of this famous queen. But the climax of flattery was only reached by Gafcoigne himfelf, clad as Sylvanus, who actually declared that " he had rather be her Majeftie's footman on

D

earth, than God on horseback in heaven!!" (Nicols' "Progresses of Queen Elizabeth," vol I., p. 517.) But even this most impious speech called forth no rebuke from Elizabeth, who was made so drunk with flattery that she seemed to know no distinction betwixt due respect and the vilest sycophancy. But the truth is, when we dismiss romance and the mythic glories which so long surrounded this age and monarch, and look simply at the facts which the official publication of the official documents of the court of this princess present, we are shocked to find what a most demoralized and vicious reign was that of the so-called virgin queen.

This gay and gallant Earl of Leicester, on whom she heaped such favours, and on whom she doted so openly as to occasion the grossest scandals—who and what was he? He was the grandson of that same Dudley who with Empson was the base agent of Henry VII. for fleecing and oppressing his subjects, and whose crimes and extortions were so monstrous that they brought him to the block. But his diabolically-won wealth remained, and raised his grandson to a position highest in the court of his sovereign, but through crimes of an equally dark dye. The only merits of this man were his handsome person and courtly manners. Hume the historian says, " This earl was a great hypocrite, a pretender to the strictest religion, an encourager of the Puritans, and a founder of hospitals." He adds, " He was proud, insolent, interested, ambitious; without honour, without generosity, without humanity. He had discovered no conduct in any of his military enterprises, yet the queen entrusted him with the command of her armies during the danger of the Spanish invasion; a partiality which might have proved fatal to her had the Duke of Parma been able to land his troops in England." And this she did after he had wofully disgraced himself twice in the Netherlands, and greatly disgusted the Dutch Government. "No wonder," says Hume, "that a conduct so unlike the usual jealousy of Elizabeth, gave reason to suspect that the partiality was founded on some other passion than friendship."

In one thing, however, Leicester was an adept, and that was in poisoning and assassination. His first wife, Amy Robsart, was destroyed by his orders in the manner described in Scott's novel, because he had flattered himself that the queen was ready to marry him, but at an earlier period than Scott assumes. Sir Nicholas Throgmorton being ambassador at Paris heard such accounts of this murder, and of the probability of the queen marrying Leicester, that he not only wrote to Mr. Secretary Cecil, but sent a messenger express to give Elizabeth the whole particulars. She only stormed at Sir Nicholas, saying she knew all about it, but that Leicester was at the time at court, and so it could not be his doing! However, neither she nor Leicester ever forgave Throgmorton, and Leicester inviting him to make him a visit, he died suddenly, "not without suspicion of poison," says Fuller, "the more that his death took place in the house of no mean artist in that faculty." After this he married Lady Sheffield, endeavoured to get rid of her too by poison, and failing, denied the marriage, and compelled her to marry another man. His next victim was the Earl of Essex; for Leicester taking a fancy to his wife, got rid, as thus stated, of his own wife. Essex also died suddenly, and two days afterwards Leicester married the Countess. The fact of this marriage was soon made known to Elizabeth by the Duke of Anjou, who was seeking her hand, and she stormed and put him in prison, but soon forgave him again. Becoming jealous of the Countess and Sir Christopher Blount, he endeavoured to assassinate Blount. When Leicester was tired of the Countess of Eſſex he intended to poiſon her too, and for this purpoſe he gave her a bottle of liquor, as Ben Jonſon aſſured " Drummond of Hawthornden," which he willed her to uſe in any faintneſs; which ſhe, after his return from court, not knowing it was poiſon, gave him, and ſo he died." This took place at Cornbury, in Oxfordſhire, in September, 1588. Leiceſter, too, recommended Elizabeth to deſpatch the Queen of Scots quietly by poiſon, a council which ſhe was anxious to adopt, but could not get Sir Amias Paulett, Mary's keeper, to adminiſter it, nor let it be adminiſtered.

Leiceſter was as tyrannical and unprincipled as he was deadly in his purpoſes. The " Secret Memoirs of the Earl of Leiceſter," publiſhed in his lifetime, ſtate that the magnificent gardens and parks at Kenilworth were not completed without intolerable oppreſſions. The Earl pretended that he had found an old record in a hole of the caſtle wall, which eſtabliſhed his right over the eſtates of many of his neighbours; "for he had ſingular good luck always in finding out records for his purpoſe, by virtue whereof he hath taken the lands, woods, paſtures, and commons round about, to make himſelf parks, chaſes, and other commodities, to the ſubverſion of many a good family which was maintained there before this devourer ſet foot in that country." The ſame volume mentions his " intolerable tyranny upon the lands of one Lane." But the caſe of a gentleman of an ancient family of the name of Arden was ſtill more atrocious. This gentleman refuſed to ſell Leiceſter his eſtate. Leiceſter uſed ſuch preſſure upon him, as compelled Arden to aſſert his rights and independence as an Engliſhman. He ſet Leiceſter at defiance, and relied upon the laws for protection; but he ſoon found how little law could avail him againſt a royal favourite at that period. Arden had married his daughter to a Catholic gentleman named Somerville, who was infane, and this Somerville in one of his paroxyfms had drawn his fword, and fworn that he would kill all the Proteftants that he could meet with. This was enough for Leicefter. He had Somerville, Arden, and Hall, a Catholic prieft, arrefted, and torture applied. Nothing could be extracted from Arden; but Hall the prieft, in his agony, faid he had once heard Arden fay he wifhed Elizabeth was in heaven. Enough; within two hours after this, Somerville was found ftrangled in his cell, and Arden was executed as a traitor the very next day. Such was the confequence of any unhappy Naboth refufing his vineyard to this Elizabethan Ahab!

If modern difcoveries in the State Paper Office had not rent away the old romantic notions of the virgin queen and her court, we might have wondered at the attachment of Elizabeth to fuch a thorough villain as Leicefter. But the great Queen was a match even for Leicefter in crime. She endeavoured to poifon the Queen of Scots; and called Sir Amias Paulett and Mr. Secretary Davifon "nice and dainty fellows," becaufe they refufed to commit murder by poifon. She was accufed of having the Earl of Arundel defpatched by poifon in prifon, where he had been confined many years for having turned Catholic; and fhe is faid to have done this becaufe, having executed his father, fhe fhrank from executing the fon alfo without fome clearly defined caufe.

The character of Elizabeth has, till of late years, been taken on truft from the extravagant eulogies of the corrupt writers of her time. She has had a traditionary reputation as "the glorious Queen Befs," "the good Queen Befs;" but the late refearches into the records of her reign in the State Paper Office have caft a dark fhadow over that once brilliant fable. And yet, if people had taken the trouble to have confulted many truftworthy writers of her time, they muft have feen a fearful fight. Of the mere foibles of her character little need be said: her vanity; her irresolution; her thousand dresses, which were discovered at her decease in her wardrobe; her being painted up in her old age, face, neck and arms; her numerous heads of false hair; or even her cursing, swearing, and beatings with her own lusty fists her maids of honour, and her very ministers, may be passed over. But the licentiousness in which she is known to have lived whilst calling herself a maiden queen; the licentiousness which, in consequence of her example, pervaded her whole court; the corruption of her courts of justice; the flagrant mischief of the monopolies by which she allowed her favourites to fleece her people; and the pauperism and crime which abounded under her rule, are matters of far graver moment. Her indecorous conduct, not only towards Leicester, but towards Hatton and Raleigh, Oxford and Blount, and the Frenchmen Simier and Anjou, it is better to draw a veil over. The court imitated the manners of the queen. It was a place in which, according to Faunt, "all enormities reigned in the highest degree;" or according to Harrington, " there was no love but that of the lusty god of gallantry, Asmodeus." Faunt afterwards adds in another letter,—" The only discontent I have is to live where there is so little godliness and exercise of religion; so dissolute manners and corrupt conversation generally, which I find to be worse than when I knew the place first."

Under these historic lights the grand pageant of Kenilworth assumes a very different aspect to that which the romancist has given to it. The tragic death of Amy Robsart, by which Scott has conferred an interest in these gala scenes, no longer hides the other and many crimes which tainted the characters of the chief actors in it. In fact, the death of Amy Robsart has been somewhat violently imported into the narrative. She never was at this feftival, probably never at the caftle ; for her fearful fate occurred fifteen years before, namely, in 1560. What we really fee, then, amid the pagan mummeries of Leicefter's entertainment at Kenilworth, is a queen of forty-two, doting on the greateft criminal of the age, a practifed poifoner, a ruthlefs oppreffor, and the very fplendours with which he entertained this royal miftrefs built on the ruin of his neighbours. Knowing this, the charm of romance fades before the ftern realities of hiftory, and we congratulate ourfelves on the far nobler age in which we live—a time when virtue and purity poffefs the throne, and when the privileges of Englifhmen, won by centuries of political energy, ftand bafed on an independence that fears neither arbitrary monarch nor overgrown favourite. What a wonderful contraft does this era of art, fcience, and true liberty, prefent to the boafted days of Elizabeth, even with a Shakfpeare, a Spenfer, and a Sydney to honour them !

It was in returning from the grand entertainment at Kenilworth, and whilft fhe was at Woodftock, on her way to town, that the Queen was met by one of the moft horrible pieces of news which ever flew acrofs affrighted Europe—the Maffacre of St. Bartholomew.

The Earl of Leicefter left his property to his brother Ambrofe, Earl of Warwick, for his life, and then to go to his own fon, Robert Dudley, whom he in his will termed his *bafe* fon. This was a fon by Lady Sheffield, the widow of Lord Sheffield, whom Leicefter had fecretly married during his refidence at court, at the very time that he and the queen were living more like married people than anything elfe. Yet as foon as he was tired of Lady Sheffield, fhe narrowly efcaped death by poifon, and, being menaced by Leicefter, fhe confented to marry Sir Edward Stafford. He was moft anxious to conceal this connexion from the queen, and he succeeded. The unhappy Sir Robert, the son of this marriage, came into possession of Kenilworth soon after the decease of his father, by the death of his uncle, the Earl of Warwick, and he took measures to prove his legitimacy; but these proved his ruin. His father had married the Countess of Essex during the life of Sir Robert's mother; she had married another man; and these inquiries were likely to bring to light many things which touched the honour of very powerful families. In fact, it was asserted that there were only two ladies of Elizabeth's court whom this accomplished rascal had not corrupted. The proceedings were put to an abrupt termination by a special order of the House of Lords; the depositions were sealed up, and copies were not to be taken without the king's special licence. Sir Robert, though he had proved his legitimacy, was politely permitted to travel: in plain language, he was banished, that his damaging knowledge might be kept at a distance from the public ear in England.

Sir Robert is declared to have been a man of rare attainments; but he must have inherited some of the libertine notions of his father. He had married Alicia, the daughter of Sir Thomas Leigh, of Stoneleigh Abbey, near Kenilworth, by whom he had a daughter Alicia. On quitting England, however, he did not take his wife with him; but Dugdale informs us that " Elizabeth, the daughter of Sir Charles Southwell, a very beautiful lady, went with him into Italy in the habit of a page, and there married him." The emperor Ferdinand II. created him a duke; and his real wife, who continued to reside in England, and died at the age of ninety, bore the title of Duchess Dudley. In the church at Stoneleigh is the marble altar-tomb of the duchess and her daughter, with their recumbent figures upon it, under a canopy with arms on the facings. In the church of St. Mary, at Warwick, is the splendid tomb of the favourite of Queen Elizabeth; with a Latin epitaph " giving him," says the guide book, " credit for virtues which history refuses to associate with his name."

As Sir Robert Dudley continued to reside in Italy, where he enjoyed the friendship of the Duke of Tuscany, who conferred on him a pension, and as he never returned to England, James I. seized on Kenilworth and presented it to his son, Prince Henry. Henry avowed his readiness to pay Sir Robert £14,500 for his title to the castle and estate, notwithstanding the legal incapacity to which he had rendered himself subject: but owing to the death of the prince, only £3,000 was actually forwarded, and no part ever reached the fugitive Sir Robert. What a Ruffian sort of liberty does this fact reveal to us in the time of the Stuarts, when a nobleman could not travel without a royal licence, and if he did not return at the time fixed, his estate was seized by the crown! The castle, or rather the ruins of it, have since passed through various hands. It was the property of Charles I., at the outbreak of the civil war, when it fell into the power of Cromwell, who bestowed it on some of his officers, who demolished it for the sake of the materials, which they sold. They felled the timber and drained the moat and lake. On the restoration, Charles II. granted the castle and estate to Lawrence Hyde, afterwards Earl of Rochester, a son of Lord Chancellor Clarendon, who succeeded to the title of a man, if possible, more dissolute than Elizabeth's Leicester. After this it passed by marriage into the family of the Earl of Essex, and then to Thomas Villiers, afterwards Earl of Clarendon, whose descendants still possess it. The present earl is careful to preserve the still magnificent ruins, as much as ruins can be preserved, from decay. The remains of Cæsar's Tower, of Mervyn's Tower, the Great Hall, and Leicester's Buildings, are striking fragments of the once magnificent whole. Leicester's Buildings, though last erected, exhibit the greatest decay, from being constructed of a more perishable stone.

KENILWORTH—MERVYN'S TOWER.

Some remains of the ancient abbey, said to have been built by Geoffrey de Clinton, the original builder of the castle, still remain near the castle,—part of them now forming a cow-house or barn, as well as the old gateway,—and the fine

Norman arch forming the entrance to the parifh church is faid to have been the chief entrance to the abbey, which was removed thither. Altogether, the pleafantnefs of the country in which the remains of Kenilworth ftand, their own ftriking beauty, and the memory of the ftrange phafes and contrafts of human life which have occurred here, make them as interefting a fcene of ruined grandeur as any in the country.

The Castle of Caernarvon.

HE castles of Caernarvon, Beaumaris, and Conway, all on this north-west coast of Wales, are monuments of the subjection of the Principality by Edward I. Other castles on this coast he took and strengthened, for instance those of Flint and Rhuddlan, as yokes on the necks of the North Welsh; these three he built expressly for that purpose, and, though all now more or less in ruin, they remain splendid evidences of his power, and of the architectural taste of the age. We have no finer specimens of castellated building than in the fortresses of Caernarvon and Conway, and what remains of the extensive castle of Beaumaris shows what it once was. Even the Welsh, who do not forget the object of their erection, yet regard them with pride.

Edward I., a warrior and statesman of the first rank, cherished, as the great purpose of his life, the reduction of the whole of the magnificent island of Great Britain into one compact and noble kingdom. This could not be done without invading the country and constitutions of Wales and Scotland, which had as much right to maintain their own independence, their own laws and customs, as England had. But warriors by nature and profession think little of such rights, and readily persuade themselves that the project which aggrandizes their own country sanctifies the most flagrant usurpations, and renders innocent all the bloodshed and the crimes which irresistibly attend such enterprises. At the present day, the general sense of both England and Scotland, if not of Wales, would refuse to pronounce on Edward I. any other verdict than that of a great benefactor to his nation for what he did, and even for what he attempted yet failed in, towards the consolidation of Great Britain under one crown.

From the very first establishment of the Norman dynasty in England, it has cast greedy glances on the Welsh mountains; and though it had been more successful in its attempts on Ireland, from the days of the same Henry II. who conquered that country, encroachments had been steadily making on the Welsh borders. As that monarch once rode through a part of Wales attended by a splendid retinue of knights and barons, he looked with contempt on the Welsh gentlemen riding on their rough ponies, and on the poorer people clad in their goat or sheep-skin garments. But the Welsh looked on the English with an equal contempt, not unmingled with the jealous fear of the Norman thirst of conquest; and a mountaineer approached the proud English king, and said:—"Thou seest this poor people, but, such as they are, thou shalt never subdue them—that is reserved alone for God in his wrath."

Still monarch after monarch displayed his hankering after a share of their little mountain land, and still more the bordering barons had made raids into the Welsh territory in order to plunder, and to extend their own already too extensive estates and jurisdiction. It was principally in South Wales that these inroads had been made. The conquerors had seized on the greater portion of Monmouthshire, by the time Edward ascended the throne, and they held in possession, though an uncertain and continually-disputed one, the greater part of South Wales. To secure the hold they had gained, they raised strong castles; and to stimulate their aggressive propensities, the English monarchs granted them large estates out of the usurped districts. As they approached the feet of the mountains, they raised chains of fortifications at intervals sufficiently near to be able to afford each other aid in any attack from the natives. Thus by the time of Edward I., there was a regular chain of fortresses occupying the banks of the Monnow, the Wye, and the Severn; these were Scenfreth, Grosmont, Monmouth, Trelech, probably Tintern, Chepstow, and Caldecot. A second line stretched diagonally from Grosmont on the Monnow, to the banks of the Rumney; namely, Whitecastle, Tregaer, Usk, Langibby, Caerleon, and Newport. This diagonal line, with the strong castle of Abergavenny to the north of it, was intended to curb the mountaineers, who made perpetual incursions on the invaders. Thus the conflict went on till the time of Edward I. : the Welsh seizing every opportunity to surprise any of these strongholds, and to cut off the English passing from one to another. But the advantage was still on the side of the English, and the circle of mountain independence continually grew narrower and narrower. Since the conquest of Ireland, the English ships were on the alert to watch and blockade the western coast of Wales, and, by the fortification of Milford Haven, to hold the port of embarkation for the sister island. In the wilderness of Tivy, and amid the fastnesses of the mountains, moors and marshes, the Welsh still held their own, and still breathed vengeance on the invaders. They would have been still more formidable to these, but for their mutual differences and feuds.

As yet, however, little impression had been made on the northern portion of the Principality, and Edward I. set himself to this great enterprise. He had learned in the Crusades to endure all forts of military hardſhip, and to encounter all kinds of obſtacles; and he now prepared in earneſt for the invaſion and thorough ſubjugation of North Wales. He did not want for pretexts for his invaſion. He complained that Llewellyn had not kept a treaty made ſome time before, by which both parties had bound themſelves not to harbour or protect the enemies or revolted ſubjects of the other; but this was as true of Edward as of the Welſh prince. He complained that Llewellyn had not done homage as the vaſſal of the Engliſh crown, which he had conſented to do, and an accident enabled Edward to drive the Welſh prince to acts of hoſtility. Llewellyn, in the reign of Henry III., had taken part againſt that monarch with the barons, and with Simon de Montfort, their leader. He had now contracted a marriage with Elinor de Montfort, the daughter of the deceaſed earl, who was on her voyage from France to Wales, when, with Emeric, her younger brother, ſhe was ſeized by ſome Engliſh ſhips and ſent to Edward. Llewellyn juſtly complained of this outrage on a prince with whom the Engliſh king was at peace, and demanded the inſtant releaſe of his bride. But of this Edward took no notice, and Llewellyn in his reſentment committed ſome ravages on the Engliſh borders. This was enough for Edward: he would have found ſome pretence for the invaſion of Wales, had this not preſented itſelf, or he would have commenced it without; but now he ſet forward at once, under the guiſe of the injured party.

After the feaſt of Eaſter, 1277, he marched out of Weſtminſter with a force which increaſed as he advanced northwards. At Midſummer he croſſed the Dee, and inveſted and took the Caſtles of Flint and Rhuddlan. Here he remained ſtrengthening theſe fortreſſes at his leiſure, ſpreading his fleet along the coaſt, and cutting of all Llewellyn's ſupplies from the Isle of Anglesea. Llewellyn and his forces were compelled to retreat into the mountains; whilst his false and unpatriotic brother David had joined the English invader, was living in his camp, and was rewarded by an English bride, the daughter of an English earl, for his treason. David was himself created an English baron, and was promised great estates and honour for his services in tracking his brother and countrymen into their mountain retreats, and for the enslavement of his country. On the arrival of winter, with famine added to its other terrors, Llewellyn was compelled to sue for peace. This was dictated to him at the Castle of Rhuddlan on the 10th of November, and these were the conditions:—He was to cede the whole of the Principality as far as the river Conway; to do homage for the remainder, and deliver hostages for the keeping of these terms and for the maintenance of peace. He was allowed to retain Anglesea; but that was to fall to the English crown in case he died without issue male; and even during his life-possession of it he was to pay an annual rental of 1,000 marks. Besides all this he was to pay down a fine of fifty thousand pounds. On the other hand, Edward engaged to surrender Elinor de Montfort.

It was impossible for Llewellyn to pay the enormous fine, and Edward made a merit of remitting that as well as the rent of Anglesea; but he delayed to deliver up Llewellyn's bride, and nearly a year elapsed before he did this. In the meantime the English invaders, by their insolences and aggressions, roused the warm blood of the Welsh into resistance. They derided the national customs of the Welsh, ridiculed their poverty, made constant encroachment on their lands, and cut down the woods especially exempt from their touch by the treaty. David, the brother of Llewellyn, amid the favours and honours received for the ruin of his country, saw these atrocities and indignities perpetrated on his own people, and grew ashamed of his conduct. He passed over to his brother, made reconcilement with him, and joined him in repelling and punishing the haughty conquerors. On the night of Palm Sunday, 1282, David, as some amends for his past treason, attacked and made himself master of Hawarden Castle, killed most of the defenders, and wounded and took prisoner the proprietor, Roger Clifford, the justiciary, and a man who, though honoured by the English, was charged by the Welsh with being one of their most cruel oppressors. There was a general rising of the Welsh; they descended in torrents from their mountains, and headed by the two brothers, Llewellyn and David, advanced to the attack of Flint and Rhuddlan. Edward had rendered these impervious to their means of assault; but they took and destroyed other fortresses, and drove many of the English over the Marches.

On the receipt of this news, Edward hastily summoned together a strong body of troops, and once more marched for North Wales. Before he commenced operations there, which he now meant to be of the most decisive character, he received powerful reinforcements, and, attended by 1,000 pioneers, he advanced towards Flint and Rhuddlan, driving before him all opposition. Leaving those strongholds in his rear well garrisoned, he took up his quarters at Conway, and sent forward his troops to recover the country betwixt that place and Anglesea. His fleet at the same time sailed along the coast, and enabled his troops to reduce Anglesea. His large band of pioneers cut down woods and opened up roads into the very heart of the Snowdon group of mountains. There, however, the Welsh in their despair fought furiously, and in the narrow defiles of the hills they presented obstacles to the advance of the English troops, which were not overcome without terrible slaughter. But Edward still had fresh supplies of soldiers marching down from England, or conveyed by his vessels along the coast, to replace the victims sacrificed to his ambition; and, determined to conquer the country at any cost, he procured the services of a species of troops fully accustomed to mountain warfare, being mountaineers themselves. These were bands of Basques from the Pyrenees, who climbed the steepest rocks and threaded the most intricate valleys with as much lightness and rapidity as the Welsh themselves. These active and relentless enemies took the Welsh by surprise in their most concealed fastnesses, and by their aid Edward chased them from their last places of refuge. Descending from the hills, no longer their impregnable bulwarks, they, however, fell on Edward's troops, who were crossing into Anglesea, with the fury of despair. They found them engaged in constructing a bridge of boats across the Menai Straits, and, attacking them before it was finished, and whilst some were on one side and some on the other, at the time of high tide, when their unfinished bridge was useless, they effected a great slaughter of them, and amongst them a great number of the hated Basques and Gascons. On this occasion fell under the weapons of the exasperated Welsh, or in the waves, borne down by their heavy armour, thirteen knights, seventeen esquires, and many hundreds of foot-soldiers.

Edward was himself still lying at Conway, probably planning or commencing the castle there, which was to hold the Welsh in check, and afford a strong position for his troops in case of another general rising. He now, however, advanced in person to chastise their audacity; but in a desperate encounter with Llewellyn himself he suffered a signal defeat, had two of his ablest generals killed, and was obliged to seek his own safety in retreat to one of his castles. Llewellyn and his brave subjects were now highly elated, and felt confident that with the approaching winter they fhould fucceed in driving the proud enemy entirely out of their borders. But the refources of Edward were not fo foon exhaufted. Protected by his ftrong caftles of Flint and Rhuddlan, he could wait the operation of other plans, and the Welfh foon found that he had a ftrong army now advancing from Pembrokefhire and Caermarthen, through South Wales, to take them on that fide, while Edward himfelf fell upon them from the north. To meet this double danger, Llewellyn left his brother David to keep Edward at bay in this quarter, and himfelf marched fouth to meet the advancing forces. But the Englifh, who feem to have had good information of his progrefs and ftrength, fuddenly furprifed him near Builth, in the vale of the Wye; and whilft he was feparated from the main body of his troops, and as he was repofing himfelf, divefted of his armour, killed him, cut off his head, and fent it to Edward; who defpatched it to London to be placed in the Tower, crowned with a diadem of willow; in mockery of a Welfh prophecy, that a Prince of Wales would be crowned in England,—a prophecy often fince fulfilled, but in a fenfe very different to what the Welfh or the prophet himfelf imagined.

This terrible blow fcattered confufion and defpair amongft the Welfh. Many of the chieftains made the beft terms they could with the conqueror; but Prince David, who had now done bitter penance for his early defertion of his brave brother, ftill maintained the hopelefs conflict for about fix months. His end muft have feemed to him dictated by a fevere Providence, as the peculiar punifhment of his own crime towards his prince, his brother, and his country. As he had betrayed their caufe, he was now betrayed by fome of his own countrymen and followers, and delivered a captive, with his wife and children, to the inexorable conqueror at Rhuddlan Caftle.

Edward difgraced himfelf by putting David to death with all the ignominy and brutal cruelty attached to the death of a traitor; forgetting that he was no traitor, but a brave man who had been bravely fighting for the liberties of his country. It is true that his doom was fixed with all the folemn formality of a parliament held at Shrewfbury in the following September, but it was wholly at the option of Edward thus to try him or to acquit him. He was hanged, drawn, and quartered, and his limbs then fent to be expofed in different places, becaufe, as it was ftated by proclamation, he had "confpired the death of his lord the king."

Thus fell the royal line of Llewellyn the Great, and the laft liberties of the Principality. There were yet much remaining ferment of an indignant population, and fome defperate attempts to revive a general refiftance, but they were all in vain; and Edward fpent a year in North Wales after the death of Llewellyn in devifing meafures for fecuring the dominion that he had won there. The firft ftep was a wife one. Immediately after the fall of Llewellyn at Builth, he iffued a proclamation offering peace and the enjoyment of all their lands and perfonal liberties to the people; affuring them that they fhould be put on the fame footing in thofe refpects with his fubjects of England. He alfo ordered a reduction of taxes, and, whilft he introduced the general laws of England, he refpected, as far as poffible, the ancient ufages of the country. He divided the whole Principality into fhires and hundreds, bringing it thus into conformity with the reft of the kingdom, and at the fame time facilitating its civil government and the prefervation of tranquillity. He gave liberal charters and privileges to various trading and mining companies, thus alluring the inhabitants by the hope of profit from their mountains; and amongft the towns thus benefited, were Caernarvon,

Rhuddlan, Aberystwith, and others. Whilst, however, he endeavoured to mollify the spirit of the Welsh by the extension to them of civil, social, and commercial advantages, he did not trust by any means wholly to these, but planned the erection of a chain of strong fortresses which should command the north as completely as the south was commanded by the same means. And thus arose, with others, the three princely strongholds of Conway, Beaumaris, and Caernarvon.

The castle of Conway seems to have been commenced a couple of years later than Caernarvon Castle; Caernarvon being begun immediately on the defeat and death of Llewellyn, that is, in 1282, or in the spring of 1283. Conway was not commenced till the following year 1284, when, finding that these two castles were not sufficient to keep the Welsh in check, Edward erected the castle of Beaumaris, in 1295. There is a great resemblance in the style of the two castles of Conway and Beaumaris—they have round towers; whilst Caernarvon has octagonal, hexagonal and pentagonal ones. The castle of Conway was still further defended by the town on the land side, being also enclosed with a high wall and round towers, which yet remain. Every one is struck with the Moorish look of these walls and towers, and the tradition is that Edward had them raised after the model of such as he had been familiar with in the Crusades. The castle of Beaumaris is curious from several causes. Though built on the banks of Beaumaris Bay, it has no natural source of strength whatever. It stands on a flat in an open country, rather commanded by the landward slopes than otherwise. For this reason, it was not only surrounded by a deep moat, well supplied with water from a never-failing spring, and also from the sea, but it is enclosed in a high, strong wall, with round towers and battlements, and every arrangement for those within annoying an enemy without. Between this encircling ballium and the caftle itfelf there is a wide fpace, fo that any enemy making himfelf mafter of this wall would have the fame procefs to commence again with the caftle itfelf, which is alfo defended by ftrong towers, and by walls of an enormous thicknefs. There is a covered way, called the Gunner's Walk, running out at right angles from near the main gateway towards the fea, which it appears at the time of the building of the caftle came directly up to the outer ballium. Under cover of this way the garrifon could make fallies to attack any veffels approaching that fide. Nor are thefe all the precautions of defence. On obferving the gateways, though both thofe in the ballium and in the caftle are on the oppofite fides, they are not exactly oppofite. The gateway in the ballium towards the fea is confiderably on one fide of the next gateway in the caftle, and this is the cafe alfo on the other fide of the caftle. The effect of this would be to baffle greatly any enemy who had forced either of the outer gates. They would not find the inner gate directly before them, but on one fide; fo that their onward impetus would be broken; their means of directing any catapult or other machine againft the inner gate would be diminifhed; and in cafe that, on the forcing in of the outer gate, the inner one was not fecured, it would give the garrifon more time for that purpofe.

The caftle of Caernarvon, which is the one now engaging our attention, differs greatly from thefe other two; and if not more ftriking in appearance than that of Conway,—than which Pennant fays "one more beautiful never arofe,"—it is equal in grandeur, and has, in truth, a royal and moft ftately air. Its fituation is very fine; for, though it ftands in the not very fplendid town of Caernarvon, it is placed on the fhore of the Menai Straits; and, looked down upon from a rocky eminence called Fort Hill, a good view is obtained of it and the town, of the Menai Straits, the oppofite fhore of Anglefea, with the diftant fummits of the Holyhead and Parys hills, the blue peaks of the Eifridge, in the promontory of Lleyn, the group of mountains furrounding Snowdon, and on a clear day the far-off heights of Wicklow, in Ireland. The architect

CAERNARVON CASTLE.

employed by Edward I., in its erection, was Henry Ellerton, or de Elreton ; and, according to tradition, many of the materials were brought from Segontium, or the old Caernarvon, and much of the limeftone of which it is built came from Twr-Celyn, in Anglefea ; and of the gritftone from Vaenol, in the county of Caernarvon: the Menai facilitating the carriage from both places.

The foundations of the caſtle are ſurrounded on three ſides by water. It is bounded on one ſide by the Menai Straits, on another by the eſtuary of the Seoint, the river which runs hither from the Lake of Llanberis. As you approach the caſtle, its walls and towers have an air of lightneſs, which deceives you completely as to its ſtrength, for theſe walls are immenſely thick and ſtrong. The doorways in the gateway towers and the windows are more lofty and graceful than the doors and windows generally in caſtles of that age. The walls encloſe an area of about three acres, and are themſelves from ſeven to nine feet thick. They have within them each a gallery, with ſlips for the diſcharge of arrows, and are flanked by thirteen towers, all angular, but differing in the number of their angles. The very maſſive pentagonal tower, called the Eagle Tower, guards the ſouth of the Seoint, and is ſo called from a now ſhapeleſs figure of that bird, ſaid to have been brought from the ruins of the neighbouring Roman ſtation of Segontium, but probably placed there ſimply as being one of Edward I.'s creſts. This majeſtic tower has three turrets, and its battlements diſplay a mutilated ſeries of armour heads of the time of Edward II. This tower is the only one of which the ſtaircaſe remains perfect, and by 158 ſtone ſteps you may aſcend to the ſummit, and obtain a ſplendid view thence over the ſtraits, the town, and the ſurrounding country. In the lower part of this tower is ſhown a ſmall dark room, meaſuring 12 feet by 8 feet, in which Edward II. was born. That unfortunate prince was moſt probably born in the caſtle; but it has been endeavoured to be ſhown that it could not poſſibly be in this tower, as it would appear not to have been built for ſome years afterwards, and, indeed, only to have been finiſhed by Edward II. after he became King of England. The Rev. C. H. Hartſhorne, of Cogenhoe, in Northamptonſhire, aſſerted at the annual meeting of the Cambrian Archæological Society, held at Caernarvon in September, 1848, that this caſtle, inſtead of being built, as Pennant and others repreſent, in about two years, was not completed in leſs than thirty-eight years—that it was begun in 1284, and only completed in 1322.

As Edward firſt entered the town of Caernarvon on the 1ſt of April, 1284, and his ſon was born on the 25th of the ſame month, twenty-four days only are left for the building of the Eagle Tower, which would be work, not for Engliſh or Welſh builders, but for the Afrits of the "Arabian Nights," and would ſeem to put an end to the whole tradition of Edward of Caernarvon having been born in the room aſſigned him by popular aſſertion. And yet tradition ſo often maintains itſelf againſt ſtatiſtics, and againſt theories ſtarted long afterwards, that we ſhould not be ſurpriſed if, after all, the firſt Prince of Wales was actually born in that little, diſmal room. In the then diſturbed condition of North Wales; amid the intenſe indignation of the Welſh at the murder of their beloved prince, and the barbarous execution of his brother David; under the well-known ſpirit of revolt and revenge which was fiercely fermenting in the minds of the natives, it is not likely that Edward would riſk the ſafety of his wife and his infant in the open town. No doubt he had ordered the erection of a ſtronghold here immediately on the fall of Llewellyn. This was in the autumn of 1282, and Edward was born, it is ſaid, in the caſtle of Caernarvon, on the 25th of April, 1284. Here was a good part of two years in which a ſtrong building might have been raiſed ſufficient for a ſtout defence : and this is probably what is meant when it is ſaid by the hiſtorians that Edward commenced this caſtle in A.D. 1282-3, and completed it in two or three years. It is moſt probable that he did commence and complete ſuch a caſtle as anſwered his immediate purpose, and that in this castle his son Edward was born; that Edward I., however, contemplated and erected a much larger and more imposing castle on the spot—the present structure; and that he caused the part in which his son's birth took place to be encased in the larger building, and that it forms an internal part of the present Eagle Tower, just as the poet Thomson's cottage at Richmond now forms a portion of the larger villa of the Earl of Shaftesbury. It may be remarked that there is no appearance of any different masonry on the exterior of this part of the Eagle Tower. Of course not. The architect would new-front that part in uniformity with the rest; but that need not in the least disturb the existence of this room.

That is our opinion of the real fact; and it is one which at once reconciles the tradition and the proofs that the present splendid fabric was not completed in two years, but in two reigns. All Mr. Hartshorne's statistical facts may be fully admitted, and the tradition of the place remain untouched. We ourselves have just as much, or rather more, faith in tradition than in statistics; for, in scores of cases, tradition has asserted itself successfully against apparent facts, and, in scores of cases, statistics have proved very delusive. That Edward I. would be very sure to preserve the *locale* of his son's birth, and that the Welsh would vividly retain a knowledge of it, may be inferred from the part which Edward meant to play with his son, and the delusive hope which his plan excited in the minds of the Welsh. He presented this infant son to them, and told them that they should have a native Welshman for their prince. As Alphonso, Edward's eldest son, was still living, the Welsh, in their ardent patriotism, fondly jumped to the idea that they would have their own principality under a prince of their own. Alphonso died, Edward of Caernarvon became King of England,

and that hope was at once sternly quenched. Under such circumstances, the Welsh were not likely to forget the spot where the prince on whom such hopes were hinged first saw the light. We may, therefore, without much chance of mistake, accept at once the facts that Edward II. was born in this very tower, and yet that the Eagle Tower was not completed till the tenth year of the second Edward's reign.

The main gateway of the castle is flanked by lofty towers, of vast strength. Over the grand entrance arch stands, in a niche, a mutilated statue of Edward I., with his hand upon a half-drawn sword, as if to intimate that he was equally prepared to pluck it forth on any menace of resistance, or to sheathe it at the desire for peace. In the archway beneath are grooves for four portcullises. The entrance on the east side is called the Queen's Gate, because Queen Eleanor is said by tradition to have entered the castle by it. On passing into the interior you observe the traces, on the two opposite buildings, of a partition wall having formerly divided it into two courts. Much of the interior is cleared away, leaving exposed one of the fine corridors, which led from one part of the castle to another. On the south-east side is some modern building, which has been raised within the old walls. Several of the dungeons are yet visible; and in one of these was confined, in the reign of Charles I., the celebrated William Prynne.

No more zealous, fiery, and yet honest spirit, certainly was ever confined here than Prynne. He was at once a lawyer of Lincoln's Inn and a determined Puritan. His famous "Histriomastix, or a Scourge for Stage Players," being supposed to reflect on Henrietta, the Queen of Charles I., who had herself acted in a pastoral at Somerset House, Prynne was prosecuted in the Star Chamber; and his sentence and its rigid execution are a striking proof of the savage spirit of the age, though it was already near the middle of the seventeenth century, namely, in 1634. He was fined £3,000, expelled from the University of Oxford and the Society of Lincoln's Inn, degraded from the bar, set in the pillory, both his ears cut off, his book burnt publicly by the hangman, and himself condemned to perpetual imprisonment. But no amount of cruelty could tame that daring soul. Whilst still imprisoned in the Tower, and after three years' durance, he launched forth another book, reflecting severely on the hierarchy generally, and particularly on the popish follies and political despotism of Archbishop Laud. For this he was further sentenced by the infamous Star Chamber to be fined £5,000, to be again set in the pillory, to be branded on both cheeks with the letters S. and L., for Seditious Libeller, to have the very roots of his ears dug out by the hangman, and to be imprisoned in this castle of Caernarvon.

But the event showed that there was a spirit afloat which these fierce barbarities of regal tyranny were only rousing into a degree of fury which would sweep both church and throne from the land. The Puritan friends of Prynne flocked to Caernarvon Castle in such numbers, that the poor mutilated prisoner sate more like a monarch holding a perpetual levee than a convict who had endured the vilest insults and the savagest brutalities of the law. Only ten weeks had elapsed since Prynne was brought to this royal stronghold when he was illegally removed by a warrant from the Lords of the Council, and removed to the castle of Mount Orgueil, in the island of Jersey.

The current of democracy, however, was running at full tide, and 1641 saw Prynne released from Mount Orgueil by a warrant of the Speaker of the Long Parliament, and received at Southampton on his landing with all the honours and applauses of a Roman conqueror in an ovation. A little time saw him a member of Parliament, restored as a bencher of Lincoln's Inn, and made Recorder of Bath. Yet, most barbarously and shamefully treated as Prynne had been by the king, he did not let this embitter his spirit against him, or lead him to assist in condemning him to death. On the contrary, he denied the supremacy of Parliament, protested against the assumptions of Cromwell, and was now imprisoned in turn by the republican power. He saw himself thrust into the dungeon of Dunster Castle, in Somersetshire, and afterwards of Pendennis Castle, in Cornwall. He was expelled Parliament, declared incapable of holding any office in the Commonwealth, and deprived of the recordership of Bath. He was one of the first to work with the reactionary party for the Restoration, and on the accomplishment of that event was again restored to his recordership of Bath and his seat in Parliament, and was made keeper of the records in the Tower, where he had formerly been a prisoner. Yet even here did not end his troubles; for his free expression of his opinion on Government matters subjected him to the censures of the House of Commons. Besides his political doings and writings, Prynne was a voluminous author, as his " Calendar of Parliament " and his " Records " testify. It is curious that in these last he endeavours to prove the supremacy of the Kings of England in ecclesiastical affairs, as shown by the public records from the earliest times to those of Edward I., the latest period which he lived to illustrate.

There is no reminiscence more lively than that of the short incarceration of Prynne in this castle. One of its earliest historical events was the surprise of it by Madoc, a natural son of Llewellyn, in 1295, and his retention of it till Edward I. expelled him from it. In 1402 Owen Glendower made a successful attempt to seize several of the Welsh castles, but was repulsed from the gates of this stronghold. In the wars of the Roses it repeatedly changed masters, and in 1644 Cromwell's forces obtained possession of it, made 400 of the garrison prisoners, and enriched themselves with much spoil. Lord Byron soon after retook it for the king; but in 1646 the Parliament regained it. In 1660, the first year of Charles II., an order was issued for the demolition of the castle; but, fortunately, it was not completely carried out. The property still continues in the possession of the Crown; and the Marquis of Anglesea holds the office of constable of it, as well as that of mayor of the town and ranger of Snowdon Forest.

A short distance from the Castle, on the steep bank of the river Seoint, are yet remaining some strong walls of a Roman fort; and not far from them, between the town and the church of Llanbeblig, is the site of the Roman station of Segontium. That martial people saw, as well as the warlike Edward, the advantages of this situation for keeping in check both the Welsh mountaineers and the islanders of Anglesea. An extension of the Chester and Holyhead Railway to Caernarvon enables tourists to visit easily this very noble and interesting castle. Camden says that in his time Caernarvon was "comprehended within a small and almost circular extent of strong walls, the west side being entirely occupied by its beautiful castle." Camden also, speaking of the remains of the old Roman fort, near Segontium, says, "On the opposite side of the Seoint, about half a mile from the town, are the ruins of a Roman fort, its walls entire on three sides, about ten feet high, and near four feet thick, built of rude stones strongly cemented together, and enclosing an area of about eighty yards from east to west, by forty-five from north to south; the west side, overhanging the steep bank of the river, has no traces of a wall. Helena, the wife of Constantine, is said to have had a chapel here, and her name is alfo preferved in a well half a mile below on the river fide, very good " for bathing little lads when they be very fick for want of wind breath, after being cleaned by a broom from the flaver." This is a quotation from an older author, probably from Leland. The well appears to have been a fpa; and the broom, no doubt, was intended to clear the fcum from its furface, not from the " little fick lad," as would at firft fight appear the meaning of the paffage.

The Priory of Lindisfarne.

 AMONGST thofe wild and ftern bafaltic rocks and iflands which ftud the Northumbrian coaft, the haunts of myriads of fea-fowls, and the fporting-grounds of fierce winds, the largeft is Lindisfarne, or Holy Ifland; fo called from its having become, very early in the Saxon times, the feat of a community of Chriftian priefts. This ifland is directly oppofite Beal, near the great north road, and now a ftation on the North-Eaftern Railway. On its northweft point, indeed, there runs out a narrow promontory to within half a mile of the Northumberland ftrand. From the coaft below Beal there is a way marked out acrofs the fands by a line of pofts; and the paffage over thefe fands, which are bare at low-water, is fomething more than two miles. The country-people pafs over on foot or with carts at fuch times, but it is by no means fafe for ftrangers. The fands in the deepeft part are feldom fo free from water as to fuperfede the neceffity of wading above the fhoes; and there are quickfands, which have not unfrequently fwallowed up horfes and carriages, as the records of the country fhow. Perhaps the beft croffing is from the lower end of Fenham Flats, nearer to Belford, where the coaft fweeps round foutheaft, and runs in a long promontory into the fea, to a point

THE PRIORY OF LINDISFARNE. 49

called the Old Law, whence the paſſage to Lindisfarne is only about half a mile, and boats are always in readineſs to fetch you over.

The walk along the coaſt to this point is extremely wild. The fury of tempeſts has thrown up a chaos of ſand-hills, and

LINDISFARNE; GENERAL VIEW.

the riotous waves have torn out caverns and hollows, and ſcattered the beach with ſea-weeds, ſhells, and drift, at high-water mark. The long, thin ſea-grafs on the ſand-hills hiſſes in the wind as you advance, and behind other hills before you the fea booms folemnly. Here and there you come upon a fifherman's hut amid the fand-hills, with boats, pitch-cafks, and old boards, the relics of wrecks, fcattered about. As you advance, the ancient Priory, and to its right the Caftle,—the two chief buildings of the ifland,—rife more and more boldly before you, juft as Sir Walter Scott defcribed them in the voyage of the Abbefs of Whitby and her nuns in " Marmion."

> Higher and higher rofe to view
> The Caftle with its battled walls,
> The ancient monaftery's halls,
> A folemn, huge and dark-red pile,
> Placed on the margin of the ifle.

As you approach, you are ftruck by the dark cliffs that gird the ifland, flanked by enormous maffes of rock fallen from them to the fea-beach. You land and find yourfelves near the ruins of the Abbey, with a fifhing village adjoining it, and acrofs a moorifh flat, at about half a mile diftant, the caftle built into the fummit of a ftern pile of rocks. It is altogether a fifhing place, with its boats on the fhore, its refufe of fifh, and its drying-houfes for the herring feafon. There are children at play, fifhermen going about, flovenly-looking village ftreets, thatched huts, and the grand old ruins of the abbey.

We ftand and wonder what in the olden time could have induced the holy fathers to choofe fuch a defolate fpot for their abode. It could not have been for the love of fcenery, it muft have been for the love of fouls. At prefent the population of the whole ifland is about 1,000 fouls, who have one refident clergyman; but formerly, no doubt, the fame of the place drew worfhippers from very diftant regions. And in truth, we may fee that a certain refemblance to Iona, the original fchool of Britifh Chriftianity in the North, probably determined the settlement of the brethren here. The very air of desolation reminded them of their northern home : the margin of the sea, with its wild, tumbling waves, and the church a landmark far around to the inquirers after the faith that taught self-denial and the aspiration after a higher world.

In our account of Iona in our previous volume, we related the circumstances under which Lindisfarne became one of the first seats of Christianity in the North of England, as Glastonbury was at a much earlier date in the South. Iona was sending forth its devoted apostles, not only into different parts of Britain, but to many a distant part of the Continent, ere the usurping power of Rome had closed the way against so simple and unambitious a race of teachers. Whilst St. Columb and his companions were Christianizing the Picts of Scotland, as his predecessors had Christianized the people of Ireland, Columbanus,—a younger and different man to Columb,—and his friend Gall, went forth into Switzerland and France. Having settled schools of the faith in the Vosges, Columbanus advanced to Lombardy. Agilulf went and founded the convent of Bobbio in the Apennines. Clement conveyed the Gospel to Bavaria, assisted by Sampson and Virgilius. The latter penetrated into Carinthia, and became Bishop of Salzburg. These great evangelists were followed by John Scotus Erigena, who settled at the court of Charles the Bald; by Claude Clement, called Claude of Turin, from his station there; but who afterwards founded the University of Paris, as John Scott, called Albinus, did that of Pavia. Sedulius, labouring in the North of Italy, afterwards became Bishop of Oreta in Spain, as Donatus did of Fiesole in Italy; and it was by these men of Hibernia and Iona that the doctrine of Christ was established in the Cisalpine valleys, and maintained its purity in the Waldensian church, in defiance of all the power and persecutions of Rome.

It was the lot of the meek but zealous Aidan to become the apoftle of the North of England. We learn from Bede that Donald the Fourth, King of Scotland, had embraced the faith from the preaching of fome of thefe fimple Culdees from the Weft, and had given an afylum to Acca, the widow of Ethelfrith, King of Northumberland, and to her feven fons, who had fled into Scotland with her from the wrath of their uncle Edwin. Donald feized the opportunity to inftil into the minds of thefe Saxon princes the truth of Chriftianity. On the death of Edwin two of them returned to Northumberland, and reigned there, one over Bernicia and the other over Deira. But they relapfed into idolatry, and foon fell in the invafion of Cedwell, King of Cumberland, and were both killed by him, one in battle, one in cold blood. Ofwald, who was the fecond fon of Ethelfrith, then made an attempt to reconquer his rightful dominions ; but, feeing the ftrength of the enemy, and the fewnefs of his followers, he threw himfelf on the power of the only true God, planted the crofs in the front of his army, and on his knees implored the Lord of Heaven to vindicate the rights of Chrift and of himfelf. Victory fate on his banners; he recovered all Northumberland, and, thus confirmed in the new faith, he not only proclaimed himfelf a Chriftian, but laboured anxioufly to convert his fubjects to that faith. He applied to Donald of Scotland to fend him a teacher of the truth ; and Donald fent to Iona, to requeft one to be haftened to Northumberland. Corman, a pious but auftere brother, was felected on this miffion ; but he foon returned difpirited to Iona, faying, "The Northumbrians are fo obftinate, we muft renounce all idea of changing their manners." As Aidan heard this he faid to himfelf, "O, my Saviour ! if thy love had been offered to this people, many hearts would have been touched ! I will go and make Thee known—Thee who broke not the bruised reed!" Then turning to Corman, he said, "Brother, you have been too severe towards hearers so dull of heart. You should have given them spiritual milk to drink, until they were able to receive more solid food." All eyes were at once turned on Aidan; and the brethren exclaimed, "Aidan is worthy of the episcopate!" And accordingly Aidan was sent to Northumberland.

At that time Northumberland extended in a line from the Cheviots to the Tweed, and Roxburghshire was part, not of Scotland, but of that kingdom. Melrose seems to have been the location first selected by Aidan, who arrived in Northumberland in 635; but he soon resigned the charge to one of his disciples, and, moving southward, fixed his abode in the desolate island of Lindisfarne, amid the roar of the ocean, and exposed to the ravages of the fierce sea-rovers of the time.

The account which Bede gives us of Aidan is like that of one of the primitive apostles. He traversed the country on foot to teach the rude inhabitants, accepting the poorest accommodation, and undaunted by any neglect of his teachings or any opposition. In time he succeeded in converting the chiefs, and then the bulk of the people. He died in the year 651, the seventeenth of his episcopacy, of grief, it is said by Godwin, for the death of the king who had proved so true a friend to the faith and to him. He was succeeded by Ferian, another monk from Iona, who converted both Peada, the son of Penda, King of the Mercians, who had invaded Northumberland and killed King Oswine, and Sigebert, king of the East Angles, and they sent for four priests to preach to their subjects. He was in turn succeeded by Colman, who also came direct from Iona; and in the third year of Colman's episcopacy there arose a controversy with the Roman church regarding the proper time of keeping Easter, as well as the mode of tonsure. This had begun on the first appearance of Aidan on the scene, as it had met the British monks in every quarter where they approached the Roman ones; but it was now raised to an intensity which demanded settlement, and it was agreed to call a synod at Whitby, before the Abbess Hilda, to determine these points. The question was decided against the British priests; and Colman, rather than fall into the Roman practice, returned to Iona. In fact, the question included not merely the points directly at issue, but that of the supremacy of Rome, which was everywhere asserted, and which the apostles of Iona would not admit, any more than their followers the Waldenses. Eata, one of twelve English boys whom Aidan had educated, was at this juncture Bishop of Melrose; he conformed, and one of his priests, named Tuda, went to Lindisfarne, and succeeded to Colman. Thus both Melrose and Lindisfarne fell under the Roman rule. Tuda died of a pestilence in a few months, and was succeeded by Eata, the Bishop of Melrose. He was the last of what were called the Scottish bishops; that is, Iona bishops; and Bede, though opposed to them on questions of the tonsure and the true keeping of Easter, takes the opportunity to pay them the highest eulogiums on their simple lives and zealous piety. In the church only was magnificence allowed. Their possessions consisted chiefly of cattle, for they only retained money till they could distribute it to the poor. When the king came there it was purely for the exercise of the rites of religion, and he was attended only by a few followers; and if he partook of refreshment it was the ordinary frugal diet of the monks. As for temporal affairs, they refused to meddle in them, considering that the business of temporal authorities, and theirs to attend to the spiritual needs of their flocks. Hence they were universally admired and beloved by the people.

Eata, underftanding that Cuthbert, who was Bifhop of Hexham, would prefer Lindisfarne, refigned it to him in 685. St. Cuthbert had originally been a fhepherd near Melrofe; but, as he tended his fheep on the banks of the Leder, he faw a vifion of the fpirit of Aidan afcending into heaven. This divine fpectacle had fuch an effect on his mind that he determined to dedicate himfelf to the fame holy life which had thus glorified the good bifhop. He applied to Eata, and was received into the monaftery. He removed with Eata to Lindisfarne, and became prior there, till Eata refigned the fee to him. Lindisfarne was a place after his own heart. He ftrengthened himfelf here by prayer and meditation, and by long and arduous rambles through the moorlands and mountains of Northumberland, preaching to the half-favage population in the glens and faftneffes whither the found of the gofpel had never yet reached. After fourteen years of fuch labours, though of only about two years as bifhop, St. Cuthbert retired to one of the Farn Ifles, a few miles fouthward, and in the one neareft to the land,—called thence the Houfe Ifland,—built himfelf a hut of ftone and turf, and gave himfelf up to prayer and meditation, like one of the old afcetics in the Thebaic defert. It is faid that he maintained himfelf by vegetables that he cultivated; which muft have been one of the greateft of his miracles, for the winds fweep over this defolate ifland now with fuch force as to carry away any vegetation. Once his friends prevailed on him to return to the monaftery, but he foon quitted it again, and went back to his hut, where he died, and whence his body was conveyed to Lindisfarne, and depofited near the high altar; but on his deathbed the faint, forefeeing the deftruction of this monaftery by the inroads of foreign enemies, took a pledge of the brethren that whenever they were forced to quit it, they fhould carry his bones with them.

The predicted invasion did not take place for 105 years, when the Danes and other barbarians fell upon it, destroyed or drove away the monks, and pillaged the church. The monks who escaped, however, this time returned and restored the monastery to a habitable condition. But nearly a century afterwards (in 887) the Danes made a more murderous descent upon it: the holy brethren took up the relics of the saint, and quitted the place, which was on this occasion so far demolished by the barbarians that it was never restored, though a cell was maintained there till the reign of Henry VIII., when all the monasteries and their cells were suppressed. The body was conveyed to Melrose, and, the monks again removing, it was deposited for 113 years at Chester-le-Street, the see remaining there for that time. The brethren fleeing thence from fear of pirates, the saint's body was removed to Ripon, and finally to Durham, St. Cuthbert and Lindisfarne becoming thus the parents of that great bishopric. The legends of this miraculous wandering of the remains of the saint are well told by Scott in the second book of "Marmion:"—

>Nor did St. Cuthbert's daughters fail
>To vie with these in holy tale;
>His body's resting-place, of old,
>How oft their patron changed, they told;
>How, when the rude Danes burned their pile,
>The monks fled forth from Holy Isle;
>O'er northern mountain, marsh and moor,
>From sea to sea, from shore to shore,
>Seven years St. Cuthbert's corpse they bore.
>They rested then in fair Melrose;
> But, though alive he loved it well,
> Not there his relics might repose,
>   For, wondrous tale to tell!
>In his stone coffin forth he rides,
>A ponderous bark for river tides,
>Yet light as gossamer it glides
>   Downward to Tilmouth cell.
>Nor long was his abiding there,
>For southward did the saint repair;

THE PRIORY OF LINDISFARNE.

> Chester-le-Street and Ripon saw
> His holy corpse, ere Wardelaw
>   Hailed him with joy and fear;
> And after many wanderings passed,
> He chose his lordly seat at last,
> Where his cathedral, huge and vast,
>   Looks down upon the Wear;
> There deep in Durham's Gothic shade
> His relics are in secret laid:
>   But none may know the place,
> Save of his holiest servants three,
> Deep sworn to solemn secrecy,
>   Who share that wondrous grace.

In this account Scott wilfully violates the truth of history by giving St. Cuthbert daughters. No nuns were ever allowed in Lindisfarne, or at any other shrine of this saint. No woman of any kind after his death was suffered to set foot in his shrine, or his abbey. His honour had been aspersed by a fair, false princess, in his youth, and could only be cleared by a miracle. Henceforth he kept all women at a distance, not even letting his monks keep a cow; for he said, "Where there is a cow there is a woman, and where there is a woman there is mischief." Even the great Queen Philippa, who had, by the saint's aid, won the battle of Neville's Cross, was not allowed to sleep in the Abbey, on a subsequent visit with her husband Edward III. The monks having discovered this horrible fact at midnight, roused her from her sleep, and, hastily collecting her garments, she had to flee to the castle. Yet this aversion did not overcome the saint's pious benevolence; for we find in his life many instances of his curing women miraculously of the most serious complaints.

Excellent descriptions of the very interesting ruins of Lindisfarne Priory may be found in Hutchinson's History of Durham, in Surtees' History, and in Grose's Antiquities. Grose says:—
"The nave of the church consists of a wide centre and two

side aisles, the columns of which are heavy, and the arches circular. In the superstructure of the north and south walls pointed arches appear. The windows are narrow, ornamented with a corner pilaster, and a moulding of a few members. The walls are very thick, and every part wears a gloomy

LINDISFARNE PRIORY: RAINBOW ARCH.

countenance. The south wall of the middle tower is standing, about fifty feet high, and one corner tower at the west end of the church remains perfect. These ruins still retain one most singular beauty—an arch unloaded with any superstructure, supported by the south-east and north-west corner pillars, and ornamented with the dancette or zigzag moulding, stretching a fine bow over the chasm of ruins occasioned by the falling-in of the aisles."

This fine airy arch still remains like a "rainbow in the sky," and is consequently called "the Rainbow Arch." The building is chiefly of a soft red sandstone, and is consequently much worn by the weather. The oldest parts of the church are genuine Saxon, with low, sturdy columns, many of them five feet in diameter. Within the ruins stand a rustic chapel and burial-ground crowded with memorials of death by shipwreck and the drowning of fishermen.

No one should visit the ruins of Lindisfarne without walking to the Castle, and from its elevated platform taking a wide and noble view of the island and the surrounding sea and country. As to the island itself you have a complete view of it; the ocean surging all round against its dark rocks; and its little area of cultivation, corn, grass, and potato-patches, but bare of trees, the winds tolerating nothing higher than bushes. Dugdale says, "The prospect from the island is beautiful. To the northward you command the town of Berwick, over an arm of the sea about seven miles in breadth. At near the same distance to the south you view Bamborough Castle, on a promontory. On the one hand, you have a view of the open sea, scattered over with vessels; and on the other hand, a narrow channel, by which this land is insulated, about two miles in width. The distant shore exhibits a beautiful hanging landscape of cultivated country, graced with a multitude of hamlets, villages, and woodlands."

He might have added that betwixt you and the land you see St. Cuthbert's Island, whose legend Scott alludes to thus :

> But fain St. Hilda's nuns would learn,
> If on a rock by Lindisfarne
> St. Cuthbert fits and toils to frame
> The fea-born beads that bear his name.
> Such tales had Whitby's fifhers told
> And faid they might his fhape behold,
>   And hear his anvil found :
> A deadened clang,—a huge dim form
> Seen but and heard when gathering ftorm
>   And night were clofing round.
> But this, as tale of idle fame,
> The nuns of Lindisfarne difclaim.

Thefe foffils, called *Entrochi*, or, popularly, St. Cuthbert's beads, are ftill found among the rocks on the north-eaft fide of Holy Ifland. They are about the fize of the feeds of the mallow, and of a dark leaden colour.

From the height of the Caftle, now a coaftguard ftation, you have a full view of the black and iron-bound rocks, called the Farn and Staple Iflands, the haunts of fea-fowl, and the fcene of fo many fatal wrecks. On one of the fartheft out at fea, called the Longftone rock, ftands the lighthoufe from whence the brave Grace Darling and her father iffued to fave the furvivors, nine in number, of the paffengers of the *Forfar-fhire* fteamer, wrecked on the 7th of September, 1838. Turning landward, the eye in clear weather catches the fummit of the Cheviot hills, and in fuch an atmofphere it ranges fouthward as far as the ruins of Dunftanborough.

The great purfuit of the prefent inhabitants of Lindisfarne and the neighbouring coaft is fifhing. In the herring feafon there is a great refort to the Farn Ifles from different places betwixt Leith and Yarmouth, and even from France. North Sunderland fends out a little fleet of herring-boats, the great ground for the herrings being fouth-eaft of the Crumftone Rock. Lindisfarne fends alfo a great number of lobfters and holibut, and other fish, to London. Of the ancient pursuits of Lindisfarne some specimens yet exist in illuminated Missals and Gospels, in the library of Durham Cathedral and in the British Museum. The one in the British Museum is the so-called Durham Manuscript, in its rich, jewelled binding. It is a copy of the Four Gospels, written by the learned Bishop of Lindisfarne, Eadfrith, or Egfrid. It is in his own hand, transcribed with all the elegance of Saxon caligraphy. It will be found in the Museum—Nero D., 4—and has been most minutely described by Selden, Marefchall, Smith, Wanley, and, last of all, by Astle. According to a note at the conclusion of St. Matthew's Gospel, which gives a full account of this most interesting book, the text—that of the Vulgate—was written by Eadfrith; Ethelwald, his successor, supplied the illuminations, which are brilliant beyond conception. Belfrid bestowed upon it a cover of silver and gold, bedecked with precious stones; and, a while after, Aldred, a priest of the house, added an interlinear Dano-Saxon version, with marginal notes. The subsequent history of this book is very curious. It remained in the church at Lindisfarne until the monks were compelled by the Danes to flee from the island, and then it became the companion of their travels. During their flight it fell into the sea, and it is said that a monk saw it in a vision, thrown up uninjured on the coast. On seeking for it, it was there found. At length it reached Durham, with the other treasures of the church; and there it remained till Lindisfarne rose again from its ashes, when it was carried back, and formed an item in the inventories of the priory of Holy Island till its dissolution.

Lindisfarne had many inmates who could bestow wealth on such objects of art and veneration. Several Saxon kings and princes retired to it, and became brethren there. Amongst these was Ceolwulf, King of Northumberland, who resigned his

62   THE PRIORY OF LINDISFARNE.

crown in 737 to Edbert, his cousin, and carried with him to the priory great riches in money and estate. He also introduced ale and wine into the convent, instead of the milk and water of Aidan, their founder. In the reign of Edbert, the successor of Ceolwulf, Offa, a prince of the royal blood, took

LINDISFARNE PRIORY: NORMAN PORCH.

sanctuary in Lindisfarne, from some cause not explained. Edbert, the king, dragged him from the high altar of this sacred place, put him to death at once, and imprisoned the bishop in Bamborough Castle.

Such were the scenes that occasionally disturbed the quiet of this hallowed retirement, when the stormy passions of half-savage princes were added to those of nature. How substantial must have been a fabric, so

> Exposed to the tempestuous seas,
> Scourged by the winds' eternal sway,
> Open to rovers fierce as they,
> Which could twelve hundred years withstand
> Winds, waves, and northern pirates' hands!

Tynemouth Priory.

HE Priory of Tynemouth was founded in the early Saxon ages, nearly coeval with Whitby and Lindisfarne. It suffered the same ravages from the Danes, and once or twice was totally demolished and left for long years as a heap of ruins. Yet it rose, phœnix-like, from its ashes, and continued till the great era of Henry VIII., which put an end to the glories, abuses, benevolences and crimes, of all these magnificent mansions. Tanner, following Leland and Cressy, asserts that there was a religious house there in the very earliest ages of Christianity in these islands. It would seem to have been originally intended for nuns, and so continued to the time of St. Cuthbert; for Virca, Abbess of Tynemouth, presented to that saint—not seeming to take any offence at his mysogyny—a rare winding-sheet, in emulation of the holy lady Tuda, who had sent him a coffin. Perhaps, however, these peculiar gifts might have a particular meaning, namely, that the ladies would be glad to have him comfortably consigned to his ultimate home. Whatever might be the original structure on this airy spot, we are told by Leland that Edwin, King of Northumberland, erected a nunnery of wood here, and that his daughter Rosella took the veil in it. Oswald, the great patron of the Iona clergy, who began his reign in the year 634, removed this wooden building and replaced it by one of fubftantial ftone; from which occurrence he has been reprefented by many as the original founder of Tynemouth monaftery. The place acquired fuch fanctity that perfons fought eagerly to be buried within its walls; and, amongft thofe interred within it, was no lefs a perfon than Ofwin, King of Deira, who was flain by Ofwy, King of Bernicia, in 651. Again, it was faid to owe its foundation to Egfrid, King of Northumberland, who reigned from 671 to 685; but during his reign the Danes committed fearful ravages in Northumberland, and moft likely deftroyed the monaftery of Tynemouth, fo that Egfrid literally became its reftorer.

In this revived ftate it received the earthly remains of Ofred, King of Northumberland in 792; but it was deftined to fuffer a fucceffion of ravages during the next century and a half from the Danes, fufficient to have deterred all attempts to re-inhabit it. It was plundered by them in 800; again by Inguar and Hubba in 866; again in 870, when it was occupied by nuns; by Halfdan the Danifh king in 876, only fix years after one of thefe vifitations; and finally in the reign of Athelftan, King of the Weft Saxons, between 924 and 940. Such was the defpair of the monks and nuns of Tynemouth— for it appears to have had both—created by thefe calamities, that, for a very long time, nothing could induce any of the religious to occupy it. In fact, its fituation was itfelf an invitation to the roving vikings to vifit it. It ftood on a bold cliff, overhanging the fea, fhowing itfelf for leagues over the ocean, and naturally awakening the cupidity of thefe marauders. At length, when they had left nothing further in Northumberland worth carrying off, the bifhop of the diocefe begged the fite from the Earls of Northumberland, and once more peopled it. Soon after this the fexton dreamed of the fpot where lay the remains of the king and martyr Ofwin. Judith, the wife of Toftig, Earl of Northumberland, fupported the fexton in his fearch; and, the royal bones being difcovered and honoured with a ftately tomb, conferred a great intereft on the monaftery. The Danes paid feveral fucceffive vifits to the coaft, took and burned the Caftle of Bamborough fo late as 995, but do not feem to have molefted Tynemouth.

In 1074, Tynemouth Priory was deprived of the relics of King Ofwin, which were conferred by Waltheof, Earl of Northumberland, on the monks of Yarrow, who removed them thither. The earl alfo beftowed the property of Tynemouth, and all its lands, on Yarrow. Yet, though it was even taken from Yarrow, and made a mere cell to the monaftery of St. Alban's forever, it became the burial-place of Malcolm, King of Scotland, and his fon, Prince Edward, who were killed on St. Brice's-day, 1094. Succeffive kings confirmed to the monaftery all its lands and privileges; and Hugh Pudfey, Bifhop of Durham, in 1196, confirmed the monks of Tynemouth in all their tithes in Durham and Northumberland. About this time, however, Matthew Paris tells us that a man got into the monaftery in the garb of a monk, who was no monk, but a Judas, and who, fecretly watching his opportunity, put the prior's feal to a counterfeit deed, which he handed to one Robert, their enemy, who thereupon began to boaft of what was in his power; but, this exciting the prior's fufpicion, the fraud was difcovered, and the traitor, having over-fed and drank himfelf, died of apoplexy, and the monks in the cloifter faid they plainly heard a voice faying,—" Take him, Satan! take him, Satan!"

In the time of Edward II., the Scots, encouraged by his imbecility, made fierce raids into Northumberland, and plundered the Priory of Tynemouth; but fome of them, being taken prisoners, were sent to London and hanged. Edward II.'s queen resided some time in the priory, and a natural son of Edward's, named Ada, was buried there. At the dissolution, the annual revenue of Tynemouth Priory amounted to a clear value of £397 10s. 5½d.; and its manors, manor-houses, villas, and royalties in Northumberland, were numerous, as may be seen in Dugdale. In the reign of Edward VI., the Duke of Northumberland became the possessor of the demesne, lands, and appurtenances of the priory; and Dugdale states the manor of Tynemouth to be in his time in the possession of the Duke of Northumberland, but the site of the monastery in that of the crown.

From very early times there stood a castle in near proximity to the priory. No doubt the exposed situation of the priory, and its frequent ravages by the Danes, rendered this measure necessary, though it could not be very conducive to religious quiet. In early times the prior, however, made use of the castle for confining any of his refractory monks; and Prior John incarcerated there William Pigeon, who contrived to put the prior's seal to a false deed. Newcome, in his History of St. Alban's, says—" During the invasion of England by the Scots, when the English army was absent at the battle of Crecy, Ralph Neville, then keeper of the marches, intended to send all the Scots prisoners to Tynemouth, under pretence of confining them there in the castle, but in reality to eat up the prior and live upon the Church. But Thomas de la Mare, then abbot of St. Alban's, hastened away to the king, who had just arrived at Langley, and petitioned him that he would suffer no one—*not even the prior*—to lodge prisoners in the castle. During the wars betwixt Charles I. and the Parliament, Tynemouth Castle was besieged and taken by the Scots. A garrison was put in by the Parliament, and the defences improved. Colonel Lilburn was appointed governor, but he declared for the king; and Sir Arthur Haflerigg marched from Newcaftle againft him, ftormed the fort, took Lilburn, cut off his head, and hoifted it on a pole as a leffon to other governors. In the period of the great French war, and during the menaces of invafion, the caftle and the whole promontory on which the priory ftands were treated by the military engineers in a manner that, however it might contribute to the fafety of the coaft, was greatly at the coft of the remains of the priory."

What the priory was in its beft days may be feen from a "platte," or plan, of the peninfula on which it ftands, made in the time of Queen Elizabeth, and yet preferved in the Cottonian Manufcript, Auguftus I., vol. ii., art 6. From this we learn that, "entering from Tinmouth town, over a wide moat and drawbridge, ftood the Ward Houfe, with what was called the 'Utter Forte' to the right; a neck of land projecting from which, and rounding off parallel with that part of the peninfula on which the abbey itfelf ftood, formed the 'Priour's Haven.' A little to the left of the drawbridge already mentioned was the 'Gatehoufe Houfe,' in the way from which to the 'Great Court,' right and left, were the 'Kylne' and 'Conftable Lodgyng,' the 'Back Houfe' and 'Mylne.' To the left, near the brink of the cliff, was the 'Gonner's Lodge' and the 'Pultre Yard;' then the north walk, with two barns, a barn-yard, a garner, three fets of ftables, and a cow-houfe. In the centre of the area which formed the complete fite was the 'Abbey Kirke,' to the eaft of which was the 'Gardyn Place.' The weft end of the abbey church, fomewhat narrower than the main buildings, as being apparently without ailes, is marked as the 'Paryfh Kirke.' North of this, apparently fronting the great court, already named, was the 'Priour's Lodgyng.' The 'Chapter Houfe' and 'Dortoz,' or dormitory (continuing from which was the edifice named 'Lord's Lodgyng'), adjoined the fouth fide of the choir of the abbey church, forming the eaft fide of the cloifter ; part of the parifh church formed the north, the ' Common Aule' the weft, and the ' New Aule ' the fouth fides. South of the common hall were ' Botereye Aule ' and ' Ketchyn ; ' and then the ' Southe Courte,' occupying the remaining fpace to the cliffs which overlooked the Prior's Haven. North of the buttery hall and kitchen was the ' Ender Courte,' with the ' New Lodgyng' and ' Bruhoufe.' The whole precinct of the abbey was furrounded by a ftrong wall ; that part of the fite towards Tinmouth, being unprotected by the fea, appears to have been rendered doubly ftrong by a wall and ditch. Adjoining the ditch to the fouth-weft of the town of Tinmouth were the ' Old Fifh Pownds,' now an old dyke."

Thus we have a moft complete view of the abbey and caftle of Tynemouth, in their full ftate in the Elizabethan era, with all their appurtenances about them,—granaries, fifh-ponds, everything requifite for them to hold out againft a fiege, if neceffary. At the prefent moment the place retains fome ftrong features of the olden time. True, the abbey has been affailed by Scotch Covenanters, Englifh Puritans, winds, weather, and thofe worft of all dilapidators, men who look with covetous eyes on fine old buildings when they want to erect ugly new ones without the trouble of quarrying and fquaring. Under all thefe influences this beautiful abbey has fhrunk to a mere fragment ; but it is a fragment which fhows what the whole muft have been, and what churls they muft have been who pulled it to pieces to build the prefent bald Governor's Houfe. Walter White fays, with a juft indignation :—" From what remains of the ruin, with its tall and graceful arches, fome round, fome pointed, and all richly red in colour, we can mentally rebuild the priory, and imagine its former pride and magnificence. Spoliation, more than time, is to blame for the deplorable dilapidation; and it seems something like a mockery that the authorities should write a warning to the mischievous, while the governor's house still

TYNEMOUTH PRIORY.

stands but a few yards distant, a model of uglinefs, built of stone taken from the ancient walls. Looking thereon, you still wonder how the builder could ever convert that which was already beautiful into anything so unsightly. If it is left standing as a foil to the architectural graces of the ruin, the purpose is fully anfwered."

The portion of the priory church ftill remaining is moft beautiful. Its arches are for the moft part round, but here and there fhowing the pointed ones, included under a general round arch. There are three tiers of thefe arches, one above the other: the lower ones very tall and beautifully worked; the fecond tier of equal grace, but fhorter; the upper are greatly dilapidated. A portion of the choir is fitted up as a church; and at the eaftern end is St. Ofwin's fhrine, reftored at the expenfe of the Duke of Northumberland. It has its ftained glafs windows, and embofled ceiling, and refembles a lovely little oratory. But in ftrange contraft to it ftands, not far off, the modern barracks. The decaying church and the noify canteen rife fide by fide. It is an odd medley of the picturefque old and the unpicturefque new. What is moft in keeping with the remains of the abbey is a graveyard that lies around it; but this the governor of the caftle, or the Board of Ordnance, fome years ago endeavoured to fhut the inhabitants out from, and to prevent them laying their dead by the fide of their anceftors. The fpirit of the people, however, broke through this arbitrary attempt. In fact, there is no place more calculated to infpire folemn and elevating ideas than this lofty, airy promontory, amid the evidences of prefent human activity and the flumbers of the dead. The fea dafhes on the perpendicular cliffs far below you, and roars amid huge blocks of ftone fallen from them; whilft the eye roves far over the ocean, beholding bufy fteamers, gleaming fails, and, along the fands, fifhermen and ftrolling people, children at play, and nets drying.

Stephen Oliver, the younger, in his "Rambles in Northumberland," fays, "To behold a ftorm at fea, a more likely fituation could fcarcely be pointed out than Tynemouth Caftle-yard; for the fea, during a gale of wind from the eaftward, breaks with tremendous violence over the rocks at the foot of the cliff by which the caftle-yard is bounded; and many a gallant fhip is wrecked in fuch weather; fometimes directly on the rocks below the caftle, though more frequently on the Herd Sands to the fouth, or on the dangerous rock called the Black Middins, to the north of the Tyne." We may fuppofe the anonymous author of the following ftanzas fitting on the edge of the Priory Cliff, mufing on fuch fubjects, when he penned them. They relate to the " Morning Star," a veffel from the port of Tyne, which, in 1818, perifhed in the Cattegat, with all hands.

THE "MORNING STAR."

The " Morning Star "
Sailed o'er the bar,
   Bound for the Baltic Sea;
In the morning grey
She ftretched away,
   'T was a weary day to me.

And many an hour
In fleet and fhower,
   By the lighthoufe rock I ftray,
And watch till dark
For the winged bark,
   Of him that's far away.

The caftle's bound
I wander round,
   Among the graffy graves;
But all I hear
Is the north wind drear
   And all I fee---the waves!

Oh roam not there,
Thou mourner fair,
  Nor pour the fruitlefs tear!
Thy plaint of woe
Is all too low,
  The dead they cannot hear.

The "Morning Star"
Is fet afar,
  Set in the Baltic fea;
And the billows fpread
O'er the fandy bed
  That holds thy love from thee!

Having faid enough of the hiftory of Tynemouth Priory, let us conclude with a fample of its traditions. In an old black-letter pamphlet, we have an account of the "The Monk's Stone, a Goodlye Legend of a Crofs; fhewing how a certayne Monk wandered from his Monafterie of Tinemouth, and going unto ye Caftell of Seton De-la-Val, ftole therefrom a Pigg's Head; with what befell him on his waie back: newlie written downe by the auctour from fundrie truthes gotten out of diuerfe bookes and ould writeings, and from ye faieings of manie auncicnte men and wiues of verie goode report."

The legend is more particularly told afterwards:—" Once upon a time in the days of old, a certain monk of the Priory of Tynemouth, ftrolling abroad, came unto the Caftle of Seton De-la-Val, whofe lord was a-hunting, but expected home anon. Among the many difhes preparing in the kitchen was a pig, ordered expreffly for the lord's own eating. This alone fuiting the liquorifh palate of the monk, and though admonifhed and informed for whom it was intended, he cut off the head, reckoned by epicures the moft favoury part of the creature, and, putting it into his bag, made the beft of his way towards the monaftery. A while after, De-la-Val and his fellows returned from the chafe, and being informed of the theft, which he looked upon as a perfonal infult, he remounted his horfe, and fet out in purfuit of the offender, and by dint of hard riding overtook him about a mile eaft of Prefton; and fo belaboured him with his ftaff, called a hunting-gad, that he was hardly able to crawl to his cell. This monk dying within a year and a day,—although, as the ftory goes, the beating was not the caufe of his death,—his brethren made it a handle to charge De-la-Val with his murder: who, before he could get him abfolved, was obliged to make over to the monaftery, as an expiation of the deed, the Manor of Elfig, hard by Newcaftle, with divers other valuable eftates; and by way of amends to fet up a monument on the fpot, where he had fo properly chaftifed the gluttonous monk; infcribing thereon:—

> O horor, to kill a man for a Pigg's Head."

That is the main tradition; but there are others, and one is that De-la-Val was conveyed to York, tried, and pardoned by the Crown; and that the monks, chagrined at the refult of the affair, erected this ftone with its infcription, to give vent to their mortification. But the fact is, that the ftone,—a part of which yet remains in a field, a little to the north-eaft of Tynemouth, and in the immediate vicinity of the farmftead of Monkhoufe,—was an ancient crofs, called the Seton Crofs. It is mentioned in various ancient writings from the eleventh to the fourteenth century, and always called the Rood, or Crofs, and as ftanding on Rodeftane Moor. It is fuppofed to have ftood at the boundary of the Seton eftate, and on a road proceeding directly from Seton to Tynemouth, of which traces are yet vifible. When Grofe vifited it, this ftone was broken, part of it lying on the ground, and a gentleman told him he remembered it ten feet high. He gives a drawing of it, full of carved figures, and evidencing that it had been originally a very elaborately executed crofs. After his time, a farmer dragged the broken part away, and then pulled up the remaining pedeftal, becaufe people trod down his crops by reforting to it. It was put down again, but again fhifted repeatedly; the laft and fourth time, becaufe it was in the way of a farm outhoufe about to be built. It was then fet down in its prefent fituation. The upper part was afterwards found built into the wall of the barn of the fame farmhoufe.

The moft probable tradition is that the monk was near this crofs when the angry knight overtook him, and fled to it for fanctuary; to which the affailant, in his wrath, paid no regard; and that, in record of the offence, the monks had carved on the pedeftal the following rhyme, more ancient than the profe infcription already given:—

> O horrid dede
> To kill a man for a pig's hede !

The fubject has furnifhed ballad and ftory. In one long ballad, which has been modernized and reprinted in the "London Univerfity Magazine," in the "Story Teller," and by Hone, Sir Delaval, as he is called, is made to go to the Crufades before he could feel "all right" after the penance and the lofs of his eftates. On his return, the ballad thus concludes:—

> Once more is merrie the border land—
> Hark! through the midnight gale
> The bagpipes again play a waffail ftrain,
> Round flies the joyous tale;
> Many a joke of the friar's poke
> Is paffed o'er hill and dale.
>
> The Ladye Delaval once more fmiled,
> And fang to her wean on her knee,
> And prayed her knight in fond delight
> While he held her lovinglie;

Nor grieved he more of his dolours fore
  Though ftripped of land and fee.

At Warkworth Caftle, which proudly looks
  O'er the ftormy northern main,
The Percy greeted the Border knight,
  With his merrieft minftrel ftrain,
Thronged was the hall with nobles all
  To welcome the knight again.

Now at this day while years roll on,
  And the knight doth coldly lie,
A ftone doth ftand on the filent land,
  To tellen the ftrangers nigh,
That a horrid dede for a pig his hede,
  Did thence to heavenward cry

Whitby Abbey.

If e'er to Whitby's filver ftrand
  Thy pilgrim fteps have ftrayed;
Defcended Hakenefs' valleys deep,
  Or roved through Efkdale's fhade;

Then fure thy weary feet have toiled
  The fteep afcent to gain,
Where holy Hilda's mouldering pile
  O'erhangs the foaming main.
                BALLAD OF ST. HILDA.

NE of the moft ftriking objects on the coaft of Yorkfhire is the ruined abbey of Whitby. From its elevation, and its overlooking the fea-cliffs, it is an object feen far out at fea, and up and down the coaft. Expofed as is the lofty fite of the abbey ruins, the neighbourhood of Whitby itfelf has many beauties. The town lies deep below the abbey, and the church near it, in the vale of the Efk, the river running through it, and its houfes climbing in cluftered confufion, one above another, up the fteep hill-fides to a great height. In fact, a flight of nearly two hundred fteps has to be afcended to reach the church from the level of the river; but above them the view is very animated, of the river expanding deep below, between the bufy wharves, and the fhips paffing in and out between the mofly headlands that reftrain the billows of the ftormy fea. Near the church ftand the remains of the abbey,

WHITBY ABBEY.

being enclofed in private grounds, but admitting free accefs to the public.

In Dugdale's time a great part of the central tower was ftanding; but the laft portion of this fell in 1830, and now lies a heap of grafs-grown ruins. But ftill the main walls of the church, with their triple heights of finely-carved windows, and its richly-cluftered columns, remain to delight the eye with their grace and loftinefs. Moft of thefe arches are pointed, fhowing a much more recent origin than the earlieft ftructure of the abbey; but there are ftill round arches that bear teftimony to a much higher antiquity.

WHITBY ABBEY.

This monastery is said to have been first erected by St. Hilda, the abbess of Heruten, now Hartlepool, in consequence of a vow made by her, and on ground granted by Ofwy, King of Northumberland. This took place in 657; and Ælfleda, a daughter of Ofwy, became a nun in the establishment, and succeeded as abbess on Hilda's decease, which occurred in 680. The monastery was for both men and women. The name of the place in the Saxon times was Streoneshall, meaning the bay of a watch-tower; but on the invasion of the Danes it obtained the name of Vitby, or the White Town; now slightly changed into Whitby.

The main event which distinguished the rule of St. Hilda was one to which we have already several times alluded,—the council which was held here in 664 to settle the question of the true time of keeping Easter, and, in fact, the supremacy of the British or the Romish Church in these islands. Henry, in his excellent " History of England" (vol. iii., p. 203), gives the following account of this most important event:—" It appears that the English in the kingdoms of Kent and Wessex were converted to and instructed in the Christian religion by missionaries from Rome and France, whilst those of Mercia and Northumberland received the light of the Gospel from preachers of the Scotch nation. All these different teachers established the rites and usages of the church from whence they came in those which they planted; which gave rise to many controversies between the English churches in the south and those in the north, about their respective customs, particularly about the time of keeping Easter, and the form of the ecclesiastical tonsure. The churches planted by the Roman missionaries kept Easter on the first Sunday after the fourteenth and before the twenty-second day of the first month after the vernal equinox, and those planted by the Scotch kept that festival on the first

Sunday after the thirteenth and before the twenty-firſt day of the ſame moon. By this means, when the fourteenth day of that moon happened to be a Sunday, thoſe of the Scotch communion celebrated the feaſt of Eaſter on that day, whereas thoſe of the Roman communion did not celebrate theirs till the Sunday after. The Romiſh clergy in the ſouth of England, animated with the haughty, intolerant ſpirit of the church from whence they came, were not contented with enjoying their own cuſtoms in peace, but laboured with much violence to impoſe them upon the Britons, Scots, and northern Engliſh, who were all abundantly tenacious of their own uſages. At length a famous council was ſummoned by Oſwy, King of Northumberland, at Whitby, in Yorkſhire (A.D. 644), to determine this mighty controverſy; which occaſioned no little confuſion in his own family,—his queen and ſon following the Roman ritual, while he obſerved the Scotch. The principal champions on the Roman ſide at this council were Agelbert, Biſhop of the Weſt Saxons, with Agatho, James, Romanus, and Wilfrid, prieſts; while Colman, Biſhop of Lindisfarne, with ſome of his clergy, managed the argument on the other ſide. The Scotch orators maintained that their manner of celebrating Eaſter was preſcribed by St. John, the beloved diſciple; and the Romaniſts affirmed, with equal confidence, that theirs was inſtituted by St. Peter, the prince of the apoſtles, and the door-keeper of heaven. Oſwy was ſtruck with this laſt obſervation; and, both parties acknowledging that Peter kept the keys, the king declared that he was determined not to diſoblige this celeſtial porter upon any account, but to obſerve all his inſtitutions to the utmoſt of his power, for fear he ſhould turn his back upon him when he came to the gate of heaven. This ſagacious declaration was applauded by the whole aſſembly, and the Roman orators obtained a complete victory, at which Bishop Colman, and many of his clergy, were so much offended, that they left England and returned to their native country.

St. Hilda, under whose roof this great triumph of Romanism was gained, was a princess of the blood, being the daughter of Hereric, nephew—or, as some say, grandson—of the great Saxon King, Edwin; and was baptized by Paulinus himself, when only fourteen years of age. Her sister Heresuit was abbess of Chelles, in Normandy, in whose convent Hilda spent a year, and then, returning to Northumberland, became abbess of a small nunnery on the river Wear; afterwards of Heruten, or Hartlepool, and, finally, of Whitby. Bede gives us a long account of the death of this famous abbess being seen in a vision by a nun, who also heard the death-bell tolling supernaturally at Hakeness, now Hackness, thirteen miles south of Whitby, and near the shore; and that, when the messengers arrived with the news of her decease on the previous night, they found the nuns saying mass for her soul.

This Hackness was a cell of Whitby. It lies between Whitby and Scarborough, and is now the property of Sir John Vanden Bempdé Johnstone, Bart. The old manor house lies in a lovely valley amidst woods, having all the air of a monastic seclusion. It was originally erected, like to many others on this coast, for nuns; but the pirates that infested the seas in the Saxon times rendered it too unsafe for them. We are told, too, in the reign of William Rufus, not only that pirates ravaged this shore, but that thieves and robbers came day and night out of the forests, and carried off all they could lay hands on. In Forge Valley, leading to Hackness from Scarborough, are the remains of a monastic cell, and traces of an iron foundry, as at Rievaux Abbey, indicating that the monks were not all "lazy monks," but looked after the minerals on their estates.

Such was the sanctity of this famous abbess, that tradition relates that the numerous fossils found on that shore, now called ammonites, and which resemble snakes coiled up, but without any heads, were real serpents which infested that neighbourhood, and were thus deprived of their heads, and petrified for ever, at the prayer of the holy abbess. Scott refers gracefully to this, and to other legends of St. Hilda and her convent, in the second canto of Marmion:—

> Then Whitby nuns, exulting, told,
> How to their house three barons bold
>   Must menial service do;
> While horns blow out a note of shame,
> And monks cry "Fie, upon your name!"
> In wrath, for loss of sylvan game,
>   St. Hilda's priest ye slew!
> This, on Ascension-day each year,
>   While labouring on our harbour pier,
> Must Herbert, Bruce, and Percy hear.
> They told how in their convent cell
> A Saxon princess once did dwell,
>   The lovely Edelfled;
> And how, of thousand snakes, each one
> Was changed into a coil of stone,
>   When holy Hilda prayed:
> Themselves, within their holy bound,
> Their stony folds had often found.
> They told how sea-fowls' pinions fail
> As over Whitby's towers they sail,
> And sinking down with flutterings faint,
> They do their homage to the saint.

Fossils, in fact, abound in the neighbourhood of Whitby. Walter White, in his "Month in Yorkshire," says:—"The fossil specimens in the museum of the Literary Society of

Whitby are especially worthy of attention. Side by side with a section of the strata of the coast from Bridlington to Redcar, there is a collection of the fossils therein contained, among which those of the immediate neighbourhood, such as may be called Whitby fossils, occupy the chief place. There are saurians in good preservation, one of which was presented (sold?) to the museum for £150, by the nobleman on whose estate it was found embedded in lias. The number of ammonites of all sizes is surprising. These are the headless snakes of St. Hilda's nuns, and the 'strange frolics of Nature' of philosophers in later days, who held that she formed them for 'diversion after a toilsome application to business.' Perhaps it is to some superstitious notion connected with the snake-stones that the town owes the three ammonites in its coat of arms. In all, the fossil specimens in the museum now amount to nearly nine thousand."

The tradition regarding the birds is thus mentioned by Camden: " It is also ascribed to the power of her sanctity, that those wild geese, which in the winter fly in great flocks to the lakes and rivers unfrozen in the southern parts, to the great amazement of every one, fall down suddenly upon the ground, when they are in their flight over certain neighbouring fields hereabouts; a relation I should not have made, if I had not received it from several credible men. But those who are less inclined to heed superstition, attribute it to some occult quality in the ground, and to somewhat of antipathy between it and the geese, such as they say is between wolves and scylla roots; for that such hidden tendencies and aversions, as we call sympathies and antipathies, are implanted in many things by provident nature for the preservation of them, is a thing so evident, that every body grants it." Mr. Charlton, in his History of Whitby, attributes this effect to the number of seagulls that, when flying from a storm, often alight near Whitby; and from the woodcocks, and other birds of passage, who do the same on their arrival on shore after a long flight.

The statement of the menial service done by the descendants of those baronial houses to the abbesses of Whitby is very curious, and is quoted by Scott in his notes to "Marmion," as thus given in "The True Account," printed and circulated at Whitby:—"In the fifth year of the reign of Henry II., after the conquest of England by William, Duke of Normandy, the lord of Uglebarnby, then called William de Bruce; the lord of Smeaton, called Ralph de Percy; with a gentleman and a freeholder named Allatson, did, on the 16th of October, 1159, appoint to meet and hunt the wild boar, in a certain wood or desert place belonging to the Abbot of Whitby; the place's name was Eskdale-side, and the abbot's name was Sedman. Then, these young gentlemen having met, with their hounds and boar-staves, in the place above-mentioned, and there having found a great wild boar, the hounds ran him well near about the chapel and hermitage of Eskdale-side, where was a monk of Whitby, who was a hermit. The boar, being sorely pursued, and dead-run, took in at the chapel door, there laid him down, and presently died. The hermit shut the hounds out of the chapel, and kept himself in at his meditations and prayers, the hounds standing at bay without. The gentlemen, in the thick of the wood, being just behind their game, followed the cry of their hounds, and so came to the hermitage, calling on the hermit, who opened the door, and came forth, and within they found the boar lying dead; for which the gentlemen, in a fit of great fury, because the hounds were put from their game, did most violently and cruelly run at the hermit with their boar-staves, whereby he soon after died. Thereupon, the gentlemen, perceiving and knowing that they were in peril of death, took fanctuary at Scarborough. But at that time the abbot, being in very great favour with the king, removed them out of the fanctuary, whereby they were in danger of the law, and not to be privileged, but likely to have the feverity of the law, which was death for death. But the hermit being a holy and devout man, and at the point of death, fent for the abbot, and defired him to fend for the gentlemen who had wounded him. The abbot fo doing, the gentlemen came; and the hermit, being very fick and weak, faid unto them, 'I am fure to die of thofe wounds you have given me.' The abbot anfwered, 'They fhall as furely die for the fame.' But the hermit anfwered, 'Not fo; for I will freely forgive them my death, if they will be content to be enjoined the penance I fhall lay on them for the fafeguard of their fouls.' The gentlemen, being prefent, bade him fave their lives. Then faid the hermit, 'You and yours fhall hold your lands of the abbot of Whitby, and his fucceffors, in this manner: that, upon Afcenfion-day, you, or fome of you, fhall come to the wood of the Stray-heads, which is in Efkdale-fide, the fame day at fun-rifing, and there fhall the abbot's officer blow his horn, to the intent that you may know where to find him, and he fhall deliver unto you, William de Bruce, ten ftakes, eleven ftrout ftowers, and eleven yethers, to be cut by you, or fome of you, with a knife of one penny price; and you, Ralph de Percy, fhall take twenty-one of each fort, to be cut in the fame manner; and you, Allatfon, fhall take nine of each fort, to be cut as aforefaid, and to be taken on your backs, and carried to the town of Whitby, and to be there before nine of the clock the fame day before mentioned. At the fame hour of nine of the clock, if it be full fea, your labour and fervice fhall ceafe; and if low water, each of you fhall fet your ftakes to the brim, each ftake one yard from the other, and fo yether them on each fide with your yethers; and fo ftake on each fide with your ftrout ftowers, that they may ftand three tides, without removing by the force thereof. Each of you fhall do, make, and execute the faid fervice, at that very hour, every year, except it be full fea at that hour; but when it fhall fo fall out this fervice fhall ceafe. You fhall faithfully do this, in remembrance that you did moft cruelly flay me; and that you may the better call to God for mercy, repent unfeignedly of your fins, and do good works. The officer of Efkdale-fide fhall blow *Out on you! Out on you! Out on you!* for this heinous crime. If you, or your fucceffors, fhall refufe this fervice, fo long as it fhall not be full fea at the aforefaid hour, you, or yours, fhall forfeit your lands to the Abbot of Whitby, or his fucceffors. This I entreat, and earneftly beg, that you may have your lives and goods preferved for this fervice; and I requeft of you to promife, by your parts in heaven, that it fhall be done by you, and your fucceffors, as is aforefaid requefted; and I will confirm it by the faith of an honeft man.' Then the hermit faid, ' My foul longeth for the Lord; and I do as freely forgive thefe men my death, as Chrift forgave the thieves on the crofs.' And in the prefence of the abbot and the reft, he faid, moreover, thefe words: ' In manus tuas, Domine, commendo fpiritum meum, a vinculis enim mortis redemifti me, Domine veritatis. Amen.' So he yielded up the ghoft the 8th day of December, Anno Domini, 1159, whofe foul God have mercy upon. Amen.

"This fervice," it is added, "ftill continues to be performed with the prefcribed ceremonies, though not by the proprietors in perfon. Part of the lands charged therewith are now held by a gentleman of the name of Herbert."

This incident is very illuftrative of the avidity and dexterity with which the Church, in the good old Roman times, feized on any circumstance by which to lay the great feudal lords and their property under its power. These three young sprigs of aristocracy little dreamed, we may be well assured, that in their fury over their game—a fury almost equalling that of the game fanatics of the present day—they were attacking a member of the powerful abbey of Whitby in the person of the poor hermit. The hermit lived, it appears, from the 16th of October to the 8th of December; that is, fifty-three days, or a month and more than three weeks. During this time the abbot and abbess of Whitby had had plenty of leisure to plan the penance of these youngsters. This was nothing less than the rendering themselves for ever vassals of the monastery of Whitby, and bound to their good behaviour to all generations. Piously as the hermit expressed himself, the completeness of the deed, as taken down from his utterance, shows how much design and deep policy lay under these words of forgiveness. It was well that in such times there was a power which could hold in check the otherwise lawless barons; but the restraining power in time needed restraint itself, and, not acknowledging it, fell and passed away.

It may seem strange that the abbot of Whitby is mentioned in the case alone, and not the abbess. The following passage will explain this:—" The abbey of Whitby, in the Archdeaconry of Cleveland, on the coast of Yorkshire, founded by Ofwy, king of Northumberland, contained both monks and nuns of the Benedictine order; but, contrary to what was usual in such establishments, the abbess was superior to the abbot." We may suppose that, in such cases as the one above, the abbot came forward rather than the abbess, as more fitted for such worldly work; and it would appear that the male element, as is usually the case, got the upper hand eventually, for there were no nuns in Whitby Abbey in Henry VIII.'s time, nor had been for long before that period. The ceremony of the fervice done by the defcendants of thefe wild hunters was called Horngarth, from the blowing of the horn.

The Norwegians landed and plundered Whitby in the twelfth century, in the time of Richard, who had been prior of Peterborough, and who died in 1175. When the abbey was furrendered in Henry VIII.'s time, its grofs annual rental amounted to £505, fome fhillings, fo that it had become very rich; and, indeed, the enumeration of the places in its poffeffion fhow its great wealth and power. They may be feen in Dugdale. The landed property at Whitby, and the fite of the abbey, were granted to Sir Richard Chomley, Knt., and in Dugdale's time remained in that family, and, in fact, do fo ftill.

Charlton fays:—"Amongft others, Whitby Abbey, after being plundered of the wood, the timber and lead on its roof, as alfo of its bells, and everything elfe belonging thereto that could be fold, was left ftanding with its ftone walls, a mere fkeleton of what it had formerly been." The cells, or houfes fubordinate to this abbey, were Hacknefs, in Whitby Strand; Middlefburgh, the church of All Saints in Fifhergate at York; and Godeland, or Gotheland; befides feveral hermitages. The abbot of Whitby was one of thofe abbots who were confidered fpiritual barons, but did not fit in Parliament.

The perfon of moft literary diftinction amongft the monks of Whitby was Caedmon, the Anglo-Saxon poet, to whom, Bede informs us, the moft fublime ftrains of poetry were fo natural that he dreamed in verfe, and compofed the moft admirable poems in his fleep, which he repeated as foon as he awoke. A fpecimen of his work, "The Origin of Things," is preferved in Alfred's tranflation of Bede's Ecclefiaftical Hiftory, and is fuppofed to be the oldeft fpecimen of the Saxon now remaining. It may intereft the reader to fee what was the language fpoken and written in this country about A.D. 670, and therefore we prefent this fragment with a literal tranflation of it in parallel columns:—

Nu we fceolan herian	Now muft we praife
Heofon-rices weard.	The guardian of heaven's kingdom.
Metodes mihte,	The Creator's might,
And his mod-gethone.	And his mind's thought.
Wera wuldor-fæder¹	Glorious Father of Man!
Swa he wundra gehwæs,	As of every wonder he,
Ece drihten,	Lord Eternal,
Oord onftealde.	From the beginning.
He æreft gefceop	He firft framed
Eorthan bearnum	For the children of earth
Heofon to hrofe,	The heaven as a roof,
Halig fcyppend!	The holy Creator!
Tha Middangeard,	Then mid-earth,
Moncynnes weard,	The Guardian of Mankind,
Ece dryhten,	The Eternal Lord,
Æfter teode,	Afterwards produced,
Firum foldan,	The earth for men,
Frea aelmitig.	Lord Almighty.

The fame of St. Hilda was very great all over the north of England in Catholic times; and not only was there a full belief in her headlefs fnakes,—

> How fole amid the ferpent tribe
>   The holy abbefs ftood,
> With fervent faith, and up-lift hands
>   Grafping the holy rood;
>
> The fuppliant's prayer and powerful charm,
>   The unnumbered reptiles own;
> Each, falling from the cliff, becomes
>   A headlefs coil of ftone;

and likewife

> How, when above the oriel arch
>   The fcreaming fea-fowl foared,
> Their drooping pinions confcious fell,
>   And the virgin faint adored;

but Charlton, in his hiſtory of Whitby, ſays: -"I ſhall produce one inſtance more of the great veneration paid to Lady Hilda, which prevails even in our days; and that is the conſtant opinion that ſhe rendered, and ſtill renders, herſelf viſible, on ſome occaſions, in the Abbey of Streoneſhall, or Whitby, where ſhe long reſided. At a particular time of the year, namely, in the ſummer months, at ten or eleven in the forenoon, the ſunbeams fall in the inſide of the northern part of the choir; and it is then that the ſpectators, who ſtand on the weſt ſide of Whitby churchyard, ſo as juſt to ſee the moſt northerly part of the abbey, paſt the north end of Whitby church, imagine that they perceive, in one of the higheſt windows, the reſemblance of a woman arrayed in a ſhroud. Though we are certain that this is only a reflection cauſed by the ſplendour of the ſunbeams, yet fame reports it, and it is conſtantly believed among the vulgar, to be an appearance of Lady Hilda in her ſhroud, or, rather, in a glorified ſtate; before which, I make no doubt, the Papiſts, even in theſe our days, offer up their prayers with as much zeal and devotion as before any other image of their glorified ſaint."

Netley Abbey.

PLEASURE tourists crossing from Southampton to Cowes in the Isle of Wight, have often admired the woods of Netley on their hanging shore, with here and there a summit of broken wall peering through the noble trees. The situation on the banks of Southampton Water, about three miles from that town, and near a part of the New Forest, is particularly charming, and has often drawn the foot of the lover of nature or of art to a nearer inspection of it. The beauty of the place is by no means diminished by this approximation. There is a forest air about it still; the trees are wonderfully lofty and fine, and many of them have sprung up in the interior of the once fair building, whilst masses of luxuriant ivy clamber the lofty walls, and depend in rich prodigality from their crumbling summits, adding a fuller grace to the scene. The visitor, seated on a fallen stone, still feels a forest silence around him; and the neighbourhood of the Southampton Water seems to complete the feeling of the monastic tranquillity which for ages brooded over the spot. Mr. Moile, in his "State Trials," has infused this feeling livingly, bringing into the picture the monks of Binstead, also, in the Isle of Wight, opposite,—

> In Netley Abbey,—on the neighbouring isle
> The woods of Binstead shroud as fair a pile;—
> Where sloping meadows fringe the shore with green,
> A river of the ocean rolls between,

NETLEY ABBEY : EAST WINDOW.

Whofe murmurs, borne on funny winds, difport
Through oriel windows and a cloiftered court;
O'er hills fo fair, o'er terraces fo fweet,
The fea comes twice a-day to kifs their feet;
Where founding caverns mine the garden bowers,
Where groves intone, where many an ilex towers,
And many a fragrant breath exhales from fruit and flowers;
And lowing herds and feathered warblers there
Make myftic concords with repofe and prayer;
Mixed with the hum of apiaries near,
The mill's far cataract and the fea-boy's cheer;
Whofe oars beat time to litanies at noon,

> Or hymns at compline by the rising moon ;
> Where, after chimes, each chapel echoes round
> Like one aërial inftrument of found,
> Some vaft, harmonious fabric of the Lord's.

Netley Abbey, however, has little befides its prefent beauty to intereft the imagination. No ftriking hiftories prefent themfelves in its annals; in fact, its annals are loft; no regifter of the abbey is known to exift. In this refpect, the glorious old Abbey of Beaulieu, whence its monks originally came, has much the advantage over it. There fudden offfhoots from the fecular world's convulfions, ever and anon fuddenly broke its religious repofe, and called in the monks to adminifter confolation to the glittering but lefs happy beings of the political fpheres of exiftence. There came the brave but unfortunate Margaret of Anjou, feeking refuge; there the bold impoftor, Perkin Warbeck, made a paffing retreat. Netley, fituated nearer to the coaft, would have feemed more expofed to fuch vifitations; but it appears fingularly to have efcaped, and to have flumbered on in a dream-like, poetical quiet, through its days of profperity.

Its prefent remains fhow plainly its date. Its light and lofty arches and pointed windows are of the early Englifh order, according with the date of its foundation in 1239, by Henry III., who dedicated it to the Virgin Mary and St. Edward. Some authors have doubted its foundation by Henry; but the charter of the third Henry, given in Dugdale, fufficiently attefts its foundation by him, and this is confirmed by the annals of Waverley and Parcolude. It was anciently called varioufly Netley, Nethley, Letteley, Edwardftow, or De Loco Sancti Edwardi. The name has been traced to *de laeto loco*, from its pleafant fituation, and again from Natan-leaga, or Leas of Naté, a wooded diftrict extending from the Avon to the Test and Itchin. John, Earl of Warren, one of the great patrons of Castleacre, in Norfolk, also confirmed to Netley the manor of Schire, near Guildford, in Surrey, which had been given to the monks by Roger de Clerc, in the year 1252. For a long time its revenues continued very small. It was, however, afterwards better endowed by Edmund Earl of Cornwall, Robert de Ver, and Walter de Burg, the last of whom conferred on it lands in Lincolnshire. But, at the dissolution, its gross revenue only amounted to £160 2s. 9½d, and its clear revenue to £100 12s. 8d.

The destruction of the abbey, according to Willis Brown, commenced about the period when it was inhabited by the Earl of Huntingdon. This was after it had passed from the family of Sir William Paulet, to whom it had been granted by Henry VIII., and afterwards from that of the Earl of Hertford. The Earl of Huntingdon,—or Sir Bartlet Lucy, as asserted by others,—sold the materials to a builder of Southampton, soon after the beginning of the eighteenth century; but an accident which happened to Mr. Taylor, the builder, saved the edifice, or rather the present ruins of it. The account of the accident is this. Sir Bartlet Lucy, who had become the possessor of the Abbey in 1700, sold the materials of the great church to a builder of Southampton, of the name of Taylor. After Taylor had concluded his contract with Sir Bartlet, some of his friends warned him against touching the remains of the abbey, saying that they would themselves never be concerned in the demolition of holy and consecrated places. Their remarks made a deep impression on Taylor; who also dreamt that, in taking down the roof of the church, the keystone of the arch above the east window fell from its place and killed him. He told his dream to Mr. Watts, a schoolmaster in Southampton, the father of Dr. Isaac Watts, who gave him the somewhat

Jesuitical advice to have no personal concern in pulling down the building. This advice Taylor did not follow, and his skull, it is said, was actually fractured by a stone which fell from the east window. The accident had the good effect of staying the demolition of the abbey, which has since been uninjured except by time and tourists. The remains are now the property of T. Chamberlayne, Esq., of Cranbury Park.

The principal remains of Netley Abbey are the chapel, a crypt, popularly called the Abbot's kitchen, the chapter-house, and the refectory. The chapel was in the form of a cross ; the southern transept and the choir are the most perfect portions ; the northern transept has been destroyed, and many parts are much mutilated. The roof of the whole has fallen in, and most of the windows have lost their tracery. The length of the chapel, when entire, was about 200 feet ; the breadth 60 feet, and at the transepts, 120 feet. The crypt is a curious vaulted apartment, 48 feet long by 18 feet broad. The precinct was surrounded by a moat. The south gateway opens into the fountain, or cloister court, round which the various monastic buildings were arranged. On the north side of the court was the church ; on the west the kitchen, refectory, and chapter-house ; and on the east the abbot's house and garden. Traces of the ancient cloisters may be seen in the court, especially on the south and west sides. A turret at the south corner of the south transept is said to have served for a landmark. A portion of the walls of the domestic buildings is of brick ; and if these be the original walls, they are probably the earliest post-Roman example of the use of brick in England. The first large building constructed entirely of brick is Hurstmonceux Castle in Sussex. The portion of the abbey on the eastern side of the cloister court is still enclosed within ancient walls.

The ruins of the abbot's houfe adjoin; and beyond the traces of the moat eaftward are the hollows of two large fifh-ponds.

Horace Walpole, in his days of Gothic enthufiafm, was enchanted with Netley, and feems to have contemplated reftoring at leaft enough of it for a houfe. What an efcape it had of being

NETLEY ABBEY : WEST FRONT.

Strawberry-hilled! He wrote to Bentley :—" Shall I defcribe Netley to you? I can only by telling you it is the fpot in the world which I and Mr. Chute wifh. The ruins are vaft, and retain fragments of beautiful fretted roof, pendent in the air, with all variety of Gothic patterns of windows, wrapped round and round with ivy. Many trees are sprouted up among the walls, and only want to be *increased with cypresses!* A hill rises above the abbey, encircled with wood. The fort, in which we would build a tower for habitation, remains, with two small platforms. This little castle is buried from the abbey in a wood, in the very centre, on the edge of the hill. On each side breaks in the view of the Southampton Sea, deep blue, glittering with silver and vessels; on one side terminated by Southampton, on the other by Calshot Castle; and the Isle of Wight rising above the opposite hills. In short, they are not the ruins of Netley, but of Paradise. Oh, the purple abbots! what a spot had they chosen to slumber in! The scene is so beautifully tranquil, yet so lively, that they seem only to have retired *into* the world."

The visitors and tourists of to-day are just as much charmed with the ruins of Netley as the monks and Walpole were. They crowd there in summer to picnic amongst the ruined walls and lofty trees, and are not always careful to avoid desecrating these delightful spots with their relics of greasy paper, and of shrimps and sardine boxes. But the grounds are carefully kept, and these unsightly objects are daily removed, to be only in fine weather daily left again; a strange desecration that one would think every lover of the picturesque would feel instinctively aware of.

A military hospital has been erected in the immediate neighbourhood of the ruins; an intrusion which for its object might have been tolerated had its site been healthy, which is denied by many medical men; neither did the Queen, on her recent visit, find all the arrangements there entirely to her satisfaction. These may be readily remedied, whatever the sanitary conditions of the site may be. The *castle* which Walpole mentioned at Netley is one of the many small forts built by Henry VIII. for the protection of the southern coast. Calshot Castle, at the mouth of the Southampton Water, on the opposite coast, is another of them, and both of these are now inhabited.

Hurftmonceux Caftle.

URSTMONCEUX CASTLE is remarkable as being a caftle built of brick, and perhaps one of the oldeft buildings of that material in the kingdom, except fuch as are of Roman origin. It was built in the reign of Henry VI., but, as is fuppofed, on the fite of a manor-houfe which had exifted there from very early times. The eftate fell into the hands of a Norman lord at the Conqueft; and in the "Magna Britannia" we have this hiftory of it and its poffeffors:—
"Hurftmonceux, a village fituate among the woods, being from its woody fituation called at firft Herft; for the Saxons called a wood Hyrft. This place, foon after the coming in of the Normans, was the feat of a family of gentlemen who took their name from the place, and were called de Hurft for fome fucceffions, till William, the fon of Walleran de Hurft, for what reafon is not known, took the name of Monceux, which was at length annexed, for diftinction's fake, to the village itfelf, and fo it hath been long called Hurft-Monceux. John de Fiennes, male iffue failing in this family of Monceux, married the female heir, who brought this manor and feveral other eftates of her anceftors into his family, and their heir Robert inherited them. Roger, the great-grandfon of John, made the manor-houfe here his feat, and obtained a licenfe of

King Henry VI. to make a castle of it, and enlarge his park there with 600 acres of land, and left it at his death to his son Richard de Fiennes, Fenes, Fienes, or Fienles.

" These Fiennes were descended from Ingelram de Fienes, who took to wife Sibilde de Tyngrie, daughter of the heir of Pharamuse de Boloigne, who was descended from the earls of Bologne, and nephew to Maud, the wife of King Stephen. Richard de Fiennes above mentioned, being thus nobly descended, was knighted and made the chamberlain to King Edward IV., and having before married Joan, the daughter and sole heir of Thomas Lord Dacre, was by reason thereof created by letters patent, 37 Hen. VI., accepted, declared and summoned to Parliament as a baron of this realm, under the name and title of Lord Dacre. But this lord did not enjoy his inheritance without disturbance for some time; for Humphrey Dacre, second son of Thomas Lord Dacre, sued this lord for some part of his lands and the honour itself; but King Edward IV., who was chosen honorary arbitrator between them, having heard their several pleas, confirmed the honour and estate to him, the said Richard, Joan his wife, and the heirs of their bodies lawfully begotten, because she was the next and right heir of Thomas Lord Dacre above-mentioned. And so the family of Fiennes continued Lords Dacre as long as male issue in their direct line continued, as we shall show anon.

" Richard de Fiennes, the first Lord Dacre, having been made Constable of the Tower, one of King Edward IV.'s Privy Council, and attended the Parliament as a baron from 38 Hen. VI., to 22 Edw. IV., departed this life 2 Rich. III., in possession of this manor, and was buried in the parish church there, dedicated to All-Saints, as was Joan his wife, who died 1 Hen. VII., and were succeeded by their son and heir, Thomas de Fiennes. He was a stout defender of the Lancastrian title in King Henry's reign, both againſt the Corniſhmen and Scots, and having been ſummoned to Parliament from 11 Hen. VII., to 21 Hen. VIII., died in the ſame reign, and was buried in this pariſh church, on the north ſide of the high altar, appointing by his teſtament that a tomb ſhould be made there for him, and our Lord's ſepulchre placed thereon, with tapers of ten pounds weight burning about it, and that an honeſt prieſt ſhould ſing for his ſoul ſeven years, and have yearly twelve marks ſterling for his ſalary, and to find bread for the ſacrament, wine and wax. This family of Fenys failed, 36 Elizabeth, in the iſſue male, and Margaret, ſiſter of Gregory Fenys, married to Sampſon Leonard, Eſq., carried their eſtate and honour to his family, which thereupon became Lords Dacre, whoſe ſon Richard ſucceeded him, and died in this place. His grandſon, Thomas, was created Earl of Suſſex, 26 Car. II."

In this extract the reader has a fine example of the thoroughly unſettled manner of ſpelling till of late years, eſpecially in proper names. Thus we have Hurſt ſpelled Herſt and Hyrſt; Bologne ſpelled Bologne and Boloigne; and Fiennes ſpelled Fiennes, Fenes, Fienes, Fienles, and Fenys.

Since the Leonards, Lords Dacre, Hurſtmonceux has paſſed into the hands of the families of Hare, Naylor, Kemp, and Curteis. George Naylor purchaſed the eſtate in 1701 for £38,215. It remained in his family for about a century, and was then purchaſed by Francis Hare Naylor, Eſq., M.P., for £60,000. Towards the end of 1777, the caſtle being ſubmitted to the examination of Wyatt, the architect, he repreſented it as ſo much out of repair that it would be better to quit it, and build a new houſe out of the materials. The thing was done, and the preſent Monceux Place was enlarged out of it. We can imagine an architect of Wyatt's taſte, or rather want of it, being delighted to pull to pieces the only specimen of a brick caſtle in England, and to erect a Wyattville villa out of it. The only wonder is that he did not pull the whole down; but it may be ſuppoſed that ſome little poſſeſſion of taſte in the proprietors prevented the utter deſtruction of this unique fabric.

The ſhell of the caſtle is ſtill finely mantled with ivy, long, no doubt, to remain a monument of Wyatt Vandaliſm. Not only has the building been ravaged, but thoſe fine woods around, which Horace Walpole noticed with ſo much admiration, have been for the moſt part felled. Still the ſituation, though low, is very pleaſant. As you approach the main

HURSTMONCEUX CASTLE.

gateway to the south, you are struck by its bold and impressive aspect. Above it are the arms of the Fiennes, with their supporters, the alaune, or wolf-dog. The flanking towers are 84 feet high, and are capped with watch-turrets, from which there is a good view of the sea, at a few miles distance; for the castle overlooks the bay of Pevensey, and presents a full sight of Beachy Head.

Passing over a wooden bridge, where the drawbridge still remained in Walpole's time, you find the castle enclosing three courts, the main one and two lesser ones. In the courts still lie great piles of brickwork, either the refuse of what was selected for Hurstmonceux Place, or what was superfluous for it; and in spring-time the ground is thickly strewn with blue violets, and the air perfumed by them. Huge trunks of ivy ascend the walls of the rooms, and clothe in luxuriant masses the roofless battlements. Hazel-bushes have also sprung up in the courts, and the wallflower has asserted its ancient right to the desolated residences of great men. Thick moss has carpeted the floors since men have removed their rushes and carpets, and nature altogether has done her best to reconquer the place from the desecrations of a Wyatt.

The south and north fronts of the castle measured 206 feet, and the east and west ones 214 feet. The Green Court was the first entered, and beyond it was the Great Hall, which had one of the old baronial central fire-places. This hall had no upper story, so that the smoke could pass out at the roof. This was the case also with the kitchen, of which the great oven of the bakehouse yet remains, being 14 feet in diameter. Walpole found the small chapel in the south-east front still retaining some of its stained glass; but much of it had been removed to very odd places, and he says he found "St. Catherine and another gentlewoman with a church in her hand exiled into the buttery."

The alaunes of the Fiennes figured in most of the windows of the castle, and the walls at the demolition continued internally of bare brick. No doubt, they had been hung with tapestry, and therefore had not been plastered; "that age," says Walpole, "not having arrived at the luxury of whitewash." But when tapestry ceased to hide the brickwork, we have plenty of proof that drawing took its place. Our great families did not fit with bare brick or stone walls. Tapestry, silk, or stucco-work gave a fitting finish to their interiors. Under the tower at the south-east angle was the dungeon; and, when Grose visited it, there remained a stout stone post for securing chains to. Over the porter's lodge was the room called the "Drummer's Hall," which was said to be haunted by a spirit which occasionally beat a drum at midnight. Addison's comedy of "The Drummer," Walpole says, was suggested by this tradition; but it might have been just as well suggested by the celebrated Drummer of Tedworth, who so long annoyed the family of Mr. Mompesson. The drumming here has been said to have been the work of a gardener, who invented the scheme to allow the midnight visits of smugglers from Pevensey, without fear of intrusion from chicken-hearted coast-guards and revenue officers. Some carvings by Grinlin Gibbons were removed from the castle after Walpole's visit, and are now at Hurstmonceux Place. There are still traces of the moat, and of a large reservoir of water connected with it; and a row of grand old Spanish chesnuts beyond the moat are said to be older than the castle itself.

The visitor should notice the peculiar character of scenery betwixt the castle and the neighbouring coast. The wide, dreary marsh-lands, intersected by reed-grown water-courses, and the yellow lichen colouring the old thorn trees that grow in the moorlands, show the prevalence of damp exhalations.

Hurftmonceux Place has nothing to recommend it, not even Wyatt's architecture, which he undoubtedly believed to be much finer than that of the caftle. It will give the vifitor, however, fine breezy profpects towards Beachy Head; and both the churchyard and the church poffefs monuments of the Fiennes, and others of intereft. Among the memories of the place are, that it was the rectory of Archdeacon Hare; that here his brother, Marcus Hare, fpent his youth; and that John Sterling, whofe life has been written both by the Archdeacon and Thomas Carlyle, was the Archdeacon's firft curate at this place.

But a particular intereft attaches to Hurftmonceux from its lying juft in the neighbourhood where the Norman Conqueror landed, and from which he marched to fight that eventful battle which overthrew the Saxon rule in England, and made the Norman barons lords of England, now for eight hundred years. The Conqueror, who landed at that fingular old town, fucceffively inhabited by Britons, Romans, and Saxons, the Anderida of the natives, muft have marched very near Hurftmonceux on his way to meet Harold at Epiton, from that dynafty-deciding conflict thence called Battle. All that coaft, from Pevenfey to Haftings, is faid to have been covered by the Conqueror's fhips, landing troops, and by the troops marching towards that common centre of action. They paffed through and over Crowhurft, the very manor of Harold himfelf; for it appears by the Conqueror's furvey that Crowhurft was one of the many lordfhips which Harold, Earl of Kent, was poffeffed of, but which, with the throne, were loft to the Conqueror. William, as we fuppofe, gave this lordfhip, with divers other eftates, to Alan Fergant, Earl of Brittany and Richmond, as a reward for his courage and conduct in the victorious battle by which he, with his affiftance, and that of other Normans, won the crown.

Croyland Abbey.

ROYLAND ABBEY—or Crowland Abbey, as it is frequently called—was one of the moſt wealthy and important monaſteries in this country. It had amongſt its abbots ſome very able men, eſpecially the ex-chancellor Turketul, and Ingulphus, the hiſtorian of the eſtabliſhment in the reign of William the Conqueror. Theſe men had a talent for governing and managing, and raiſed the monaſtery to a height of great reputation and power.

Croyland was built on a great bog in the fens of the Lincolnſhire Holland. It was on an iſland lying between a number of ſtreams, ſtruggling towards the Waſh, between the main ſtreams of the Welland and the Nen. Brompton, in deſcribing the marſhland of Croyland, ſays:—"Eſt autem palus illa, de qua loquimur, latiſſima et viſu decora, multis fluviis et inſulis decurrentibus irrigata, multis lacubus magnis et parvis dilata, multis etiam ſylvis inſulis florida et amœna, infra quam abbatiæ de Ely, Chateris, Thorneye, et Crouland ſituantur: ſed juxta eam abbatiæ de Burgh et Spaulding, eccleſia ſancti Ivonis ſuper vocam fluvium Huntingdon, et eccleſia ſancti Egidii ſuper Grentam fluvium Cantabrigiæ ſtatuuntur." It was a vaſt watery region of ſtreams, lakes, woods, principally, it may be preſumed, of alders and willows, of rank vegetation and wild fowl, with plenty of fat eels. In this tottering and quagmire waste did the Saxon monks lay the foundations of Croyland, Ely, Thorney, Chateris, and Peterborough, having a prophetic sense that, as this unctuous district of fish and frogs, reeds and bulrushes, became drained, it would become eminently rich. Another motive, no doubt, was to avoid the visits of the Danes, who might find such places as Lindisfarne and Whitby, on their solid rocks, more accessible, and might not care to drag their vessels up the sluggish streams of Lincolnshire, or to wade amid its mud after these half-aquatic nests of monks.

It was one of the fancies of these old devotees to select a spot for their religious meditations where nobody else could or would live. In this oozy and flaggy fenland, amid the dark, glossy alder trees, and the whispering of reeds, with the wild duck, the water-hen, and the flitting dragon-fly, a young warrior, of high family connexions, renouncing his military profession, and assuming the ecclesiastical habit, had built his solitary hut, and sought a way to heaven at a distance from the elbowings of man. Guthlac, this soldier no longer of any earthly king, but become the soldier of Christ, and fighting his battles alone with the invisible enemies of man, soon became, however, famous for his sanctity and his prophetic gifts. To him fled Ethelbald, a Saxon earl, and great nephew of Penda, being pursued by his cousin Ceolred, who then governed Mercia. Guthlac not only comforted Ethelbald, but assured him that he would undoubtedly live to wear the crown of Mercia, and that without any trouble, any battle, or any bloodshed. Improbable as this seemed, it all came to pass; and Ethelbald, mindful of his vow to build a monastery on the site of Guthlac's cell if these assurances were verified, proceeded in 716 to fulfil his promise. Guthlac had departed this life; but he showed Ethelbald that he was equally attentive to this engagement, by appearing to him, and pointing out the exact spot for the erection of the sacred fane. It was just as unlikely a situation for a building as could be imagined. It was a deep and watery swamp; but Ethelbald caused great numbers of the neighbouring alders to be cut down, and driven into the spongy mass. On this was raised a building of wood, but not before hundreds of boat-loads of dry earth had been brought from a distance of nine miles to make a solid surface or floor for the monastery. Ethelbald then sent for Kenulph, a monk of Evesham, and conveyed the island of Croyland to him and his monks for ever, describing all the boundaries in a charter, and giving three hundred pounds down, and a hundred a-year for ten years, towards the erection of the building. When this was finished, the remains of Guthlac were conveyed into the church, and buried with great ceremony near the high altar, where they continued to perform many miracles. At the time of the building of Croyland there were four other hermits inhabiting cells on this marshy island, who were permitted by the abbot Kenulph to finish their days there; and Pega, the sister of Guthlac, was also an anchoritess on the island; but she brought to the monastery the sacred treasures possessed by Guthlac, namely, his psalter, and the whip of St. Bartholomew, which figures, along with three knives, in the arms of Croyland still. She brought other relics, and, putting them into the hands of Kenulph, retired to her cell at about two miles distance from the monastery, when, after an abode of two years and three months, she went to Rome and there ended her life.

Notwithstanding the quagmire character of the place, monks flocked to it, and men of substance conferred affluence on it. Kings who, like Ethelbald, in the days of their adversity, had fought refuge there, gave them gifts and privileges. Witlaf, who had concealed himself there from the pursuit of King Egbert, on becoming king himself, gave a fresh charter to Croyland in 833, and granted the privilege of sanctuary betwixt the five waters of Croyland. He bestowed also on the monastery his coronation robe, to be made into a cope or casula; a golden veil, embroidered with the Fall of Troy, to be suspended on the walls on the day of his anniversary; a golden cup with figures of vine-dressers fighting with dragons, called his crucibolum, and his drinking horn. In the following reign, however, the brother of Witlaf stripped the monastery of

CROYLAND ABBEY: WESTERN FRONT.

its jewels and gold ; and, in the ninth century, the Danes not only plundered the monastery, and murdered the monks, but burnt down the church, the convent, and its offices.

The monastery continued for a long time in ruins ; but, in 946, as Turketul, the chancellor of King Edred, was on his way into Northumberland to quell a rebellion there, he happened to take his way by Croyland, where he found three old monks who had escaped the massacre of the Danes, and the oppressive hand of King Beorred, who had seized on the sacred lands. These monks had constructed a little oratory within the ruins, where they received the great chancellor in the best manner they could, showed him the relics of St. Guthlac, and related to him the story of their misfortunes. The chancellor was greatly affected by their humble piety, their sorrows, and their hospitality. After putting down the northern rebellion, he again took Croyland in his way, and gave the monks twenty pounds in silver. On his return to court, he extolled everywhere the generous behaviour of the monks in their deep adversity, so that " Croyland courtesy " became a phrase. The king, on hearing of the calamities of Croyland, gave Turketul full licence to do whatever he thought necessary for the restoration of the monastery. After this Turketul declared his intention of assuming the cowl and retiring himself to Croyland. The king did all in his power to dissuade him from this design, but, finding it vain, he accompanied him to Croyland. Turketul made over to the king all his manors, which were more than sixty, reserving only every tenth ; and those six manors which lay near Croyland he conferred on the abbey. At this royal visit two of the monks, who had fled to Winchester from the Danes, Bruno and Aio, were recalled. Turketul was appointed abbot. He now liberated the manors of the monastery, which were in debt, and the king gave a new charter to it. Many learned men followed Turketul to Croyland. The church and monaftery were rebuilt about 950; and alfo a cell at Pegaland dedicated to the virgin, St. Pega, on the eaft fide of the monaftery, in which he placed fuch perfons as wifhed to join the brethren, till they had received fair trial of their characters and progrefs in piety. Some of thefe continued feculars, fome became priefts, others clerks. Turketul, by the aid of Aio, who was an eminent civilian, and Thurgar, who had been at Croyland from his youth, drew up the hiftory of the abbey, from its foundation to the fourteenth year of King Edgar. He then divided the brethren into three different ranks, according to the time they had been in the monaftery, affigning them their particular duties. The third and fenior clafs confifted of men who had reached their fiftieth year. They were called Sempactæ, or privileged perfons, and were exempted from all offices in the houfe, except by particular command of the abbot. Each had his own chamber, with a junior brother to keep him company, and a clerk or boy to wait on him. There has been much difcuffion on this word Sempacta, and Du Cange fuppofes it to mean, not that thefe monks were Sympactæ, but had συμπακται, or junior monks, to attend on them.

Having brought Croyland into admirable order, and made it a model among monafteries, Turketul died at the age of fixty-eight, having been abbot twenty-feven years. Turketul's conftitution had fuffered much from bodily wounds, received in early life; and thus he reached only a moderate age for an inmate of Croyland; for, contrary as it may feem to our notions of the unhealthinefs of low and damp fituations, the monks of Croyland frequently attained amazing ages. One of them, Clarenbaldus, was a hundred and fixty-eight at the time of his deceafe. Swarlingus, another monk, was a hundred and forty-two; and Turgarus, a third, a hundred and thirteen. Brunus and Aio were very old. On his death-bed Turketul called together the whole of the brethren, and made the steward read to them the exact amount of the property, furniture, and treasures, both in money and relics, of the monastery, that the steward might be answerable for these after his death. The money itself amounted to six thousand pounds. He also warned them expressly and repeatedly to take especial care of their fire. This was afterwards deemed prophetic, for the abbey was burnt down in the time of Ingulphus.

From this period (975) to the Norman Conquest, the fortunes of Croyland were various, sometimes receiving rich benefactions, sometimes stripped by the Danes under Turkel, Swane, and others. With the Conquest came a severe trial to the monks. Wulketul was then abbot; and Ivo Tailbois, the Norman, married the sister of the Saxon earls Edwin and Morcar, became the lord of Hoyland, or Holland, ravaged the lands of the monks, and maimed their cattle. His malevolence was inflamed by the honour paid by the brethren of Croyland to the name and remains of the great Saxon earl, Waltheof, who had been a great benefactor to them. Wulketul irritated Tailbois still more by publishing an account of the miracles performed at Waltheof's tomb, in the chapter-house of Croyland. He was summoned before a council in London, 1075, accused of idolatry, and committed to prison at Glastonbury, "sub cruentissimo tum abbate Thurstano, procul a notis et a sua patria." The treasure of the abbey was, at the same time, confiscated to the king.

Walketul being thus deposed, William the Conqueror appointed to the abbacy Ingulphus, who became the historian, and the most efficient head of the monastery since the days of Turketul. He was a favourite of King William, having been at court in 1051, when William paid his visit to Edward the Confessor, and so much attracted William's regard, that he invited him to accompany him to Normandy, and made him his secretary. Ingulphus afterwards set out with thirty knights and clerks on a pilgrimage to the Holy Land. They had the ill fortune to be attacked and plundered by the Arabs before arriving at Jerusalem. They managed, however, to reach the Holy City, and saw the Church of the Holy Sepulchre, but were prevented visiting any other of the sacred places by the Arabs. They reached home, reduced to two-thirds of their number, and in the most deplorable state of wretchedness. Ingulphus retired to the Abbey of Fontenelle, where he became prior. When Duke William embarked for England, he brought him from his abbot twelve chosen horsemen, and a hundred marks for their pay; and William not only gave in return the vineyard Cari Loci to the Abbey of Fontenelle, but, on the deposition of Wulketul, sent for Ingulphus, and made him abbot of Croyland.

Ingulphus found the affairs of the abbey in great disorder. The monks amounted to sixty-two, but four were lay brethren; and there were more than a hundred monks from other monasteries residing there, who were called "comprofessi." These were from Thorney, Peterborough, Ely, St. Edmundsbury, and places as distant as St. Albans, Westminster, Norwich, and even York. They came and went as they pleased, staying half a year, or a year, and then returning to their own monastery again. The plea for this was the troubled state of the times, and the necessity of seeking a place of security. But we may suppose that there was a good deal of licence in the practice; and Ingulphus, accordingly, found the affairs of the convent in a very ruinous state. The steward had grown enormously rich, and, when Ingulphus examined into his accounts, he claimed Helieftone, one of the manors, as his own. Ingulphus brought the matter before the king's judges at Stamford; and as Afhford, this unjuft fteward, was riding thither on the day appointed, his horfe threw him and broke his neck. This was regarded as a clearly divine judgment; but this was not all. As the body of Afhford was carried in his coffin to burial at Peterborough, a fudden darknefs and heavy rain fell on the proceffion; the coffin was thrown violently from the bearers' fhoulders, was broken open, and the corpfe rolled out on the muddy ground, where it was fuffered to lie a confiderable time, no one daring to approach it. Thefe awful events fettled the queftion, not only of the right of the monaftery to Helieftone; but thenceforward, fays Ingulphus, no one ever again dared to encroach on the patrimony of St. Guthlac.

From this period to the diffolution, the monaftery enjoyed a ftate of great profperity. Ingulphus went up to London to folicit the king on many accounts. The firft matter was highly creditable to him. It was to pray William to remit the punifhment of Wulketul, and allow him to return to Croyland. William reftored him to liberty, but forbade him to approach Croyland except on fpecial invitation from Ingulphus himfelf. Ingulphus, however, found frequent occafion to invite him thither, on the plea of confulting him on matters connected with the rights of the monaftery, on which no prior was fo well informed, and thus he added much to the comfort of the old abbot during the remainder of his days. Ingulphus alfo laid claim to many parts of the poffeffions of the convent which had been ufurped by the new lords of the land, and fucceeded againft all but the too powerful Ivo Tailbois, who ftill kept faft hold on the manor of Spalding; but Ingulphus left a ftrict charge to his fucceffors to affert their right to it on all poffible occafions. A few days after his return home, we are told that "the winter fet in with unufual feverity. The provifions of the convent failed; the fens were fo bound up with ice, that nothing could be conveyed from the neighbouring manors. In this extremity, Abbot Ingulphus betook himfelf to prayer for a whole night before St. Guthlac's fhrine. In the morning, while the convent was at prayers in the church, a voice was fuddenly heard from the north part of the monaftery, as of an angel faying, 'Accipite victualia fratribus, et parate panes ut manducent hii.' The whole convent running out, no perfon could be feen; but four large facks, two of wheat and two of flour, were ftanding in readinefs in the church-yard."

But, relieved miraculoufly from one difficulty, Ingulphus found himfelf in another. The Conqueror was dead, William Rufus was on the throne, and the infatiable Tailbois, who was in favour with the king, feized on all the lands of the abbey within his demefne, at Cappelade, Spalding, Pyncebeck, and Algare. Ingulphus tried the mediation of Richard de Rulos and other friends, but without avail; and he then reforted to Archbifhop Lanfranc, to whom he exhibited the title to the abbey lands, and who boldly ordered the Sheriff of Lincoln to compel reftoration. But the flood of the misfortunes of Croyland had not reached its height. In 1091, four years after Tailbois was compelled to difgorge the abbey lands, a fire broke out in the monaftery, through the careleffnefs of a plumber, and confumed the greater part of the fabric and many of the charters. No fooner was this known than many powerful friends fent in provifions and money for the prefent fupport of the monks and the rebuilding of the convent. But the news was alfo fpecially delightful to the greedy Ivo Tailbois, who hoped that there was an end to the title-deeds of the lands he coveted. But thefe had efcaped, and this Norman harpy was difappointed. He then fet on ruffians to waylay the clerk of Trigus (who had produced the deeds at Spalding) who feized and fearched him; but they were again difappointed, for the wary clerk had fent them another way. From that time Ingulphus kept the furviving charters in great fecrecy; and foon after Tailbois was accufed of confpiring againft the king, and outlawed; and thus the convent was relieved of his perfecutions.

Ingulphus clofed his diftinguifhed career in 1109, and was buried with all honour in the chapter-houfe. Joffrid, the prior of St. Ebrulph, in Normandy, fucceeded him, and began rebuilding the monaftery. For this purpofe indulgences were liberally granted, and the monks travelled with them over Wales, Ireland, Cornwall, Denmark, Norway, France, Flanders, and Scotland. Other monks, very learned men—Gilbert, Odo, and William—proceeded to Cambridge, and delivered lectures on grammar, rhetoric, and logic, on Tully and Quintillian, and preached alfo on Sundays and Saints' days in Englifh, Latin, and French, and againft the Jews. Their lectures were exceedingly popular, and greatly aided the building fund. In the year 1114, Joffrid laid the firft ftone of the new building, and was followed by many diftinguifhed perfons, both gentlemen and ladies, who each laid a ftone, and then a contribution upon it. Some laid down money, fome an order for a quarrier, a mafon, or a carpenter, to work on the building at their expenfe; others laid down the title to the patronage of different churches. Thefe, of courfe, were barons, knights, and ladies of great eftate. The bafes of each pillar were laid by companies of workmen, fifty and fixty in number, who each offered one day's work in a month till the whole fhould be finifhed. Or they were laid by the prieft, deacon, and men of different parifhes, who gave wheat, or malt, or the quarrying and carriage of ftone, or money to an equal value. Whilft they laid the different ftones, the Abbot

Joffrid delivered a difcourfe to each party, and then invited them to attend prayers, and afterwards to dinner. The abbots of Croyland and Thorney, with near four hundred monks of different monafteries, dined in the refectory; the two earls and two barons, with their wives, the knights and gentlemen, dined in the abbot's hall; the fix companies who raifed the fix pillars, with their wives, in the cloifter; and the populace in the court; the whole amounting to more than five thoufand perfons.

Three years later, whilft the building was in progrefs, and the roof not yet on, came an earthquake, cracked the new walls fo that they had to be fhored up with beams, and threw much of them down. Scarcely was the place finifhed, when it was burnt down again, and for the third time. The undaunted monks, however, fet zealoufly to work, and once more rebuilt it in a very magnificent ftyle; and William de Croyland, fome years afterwards, made great additions to it.

Croyland was nearly related with the fate of the mad tyrant, King John. In the year 1216, when feverely preffed by the barons and their ally the Dauphin Louis of France, John, in the autumn of that year, made himfelf mafter of Lincoln; and, taking up his head-quarters there, made many a predatory excurfion into the country round for fupplies, and for doing all poffible damage to thofe who favoured the barons. His efpecial hatred fell on the Church, and on monafteries, from the great part which the Pope and Archbifhop Langton had taken againft him. The latter, indeed, had ftirred up the barons to their oppofition, and drawn the great charter which they compelled him to fign at Runnymede. At the beginning of October he marched through Peterborough, entered the diftrict of Croyland, and plundered and burnt the farm-houfes belonging to the abbey. Thence he croffed over to Lynn, and, turning againſt Wiſbeach, and attempting to croſs the ſouthern ſide of the Waſh by the ſands, at low water, at a place called the Croſs Keys, he was overtaken by the tide before he reached the Foſs Dyke, and had a great number of his men, his wagons and ſumpter horſes carrying his baggage and money, ſwept away. All the world knows the miſerable end that he made. Coming direct from the plunder of religious houſes, he was compelled to ſeek refuge at Swineſhead Abbey, where he paſſed the night. Here he ate voraciouſly of peaches, or pears, and the next day was exceſſively ill. Tradition ſays that a monk aided his own gluttony by a doſe of poiſon; but this is not recorded by any writer within half a century of the time, and probably was not needed to produce his death. His mortification at the loſs of his baggage and troops, and his voracity, were, it may be ſuppoſed, enough to kill him. Travelling in great agony in a litter, he reached Newark, and there died.

During the wars of York and Lancaſter, the unfortunate Henry VI. paid a viſit to the tomb of St. Guthlac, and ſpent three days and three nights at the abbey, and was ſo charmed with the monaſtic life, that he deſired to be admitted into the fraternity, and in return for this favour he granted the abbey a new charter of liberties. How exactly is this diſpoſition portrayed by Shakſpeare, when he makes Henry exclaim :—

> Oh God! methinks it were a happy life,
> To be no better than a homely ſwain,
> To ſit upon a hill as I do now,
> To carve out dials quaintly, point by point,
> Thereby to ſee the minutes how they run.
> *   *   *   *   *
> So many minutes, hours, days, weeks, months, and years,
> Paſſed over to the end they were created,
> Would bring white hairs unto a quiet grave.
> Ah! what a life were this! how ſweet! how lovely!

> Gives not the hawthorn bush a sweeter shade
> To shepherds looking on their silly sheep,
> Than doth a rich embroidered canopy
> To kings that fear their subjects' treachery?
> O yes, it doth, a thousandfold it doth!

This shows a spirit that would have found a heaven in the peaceful contemplations of the cloister. Henry was a monk set by a cross fate on a throne.

In 1464, Croyland had again great inmates. Margaret, Duchess of Somerset, and her daughter Margaret, the Countess of Richmond, are recorded to have been received into the sisterhood of Croyland.

The revenues of the abbey at the dissolution show that, in spite of all its greedy aristocratic neighbours, Croyland had managed to continue rich. Its gross revenue, according to Speed, was £1,217 5s. 11d.; its net income, according to Stevens and Tanner, £1,083 15s. 10½d. The east part of the church, with the transepts, was taken down soon after the dissolution; but the nave and the aisles left standing as a parish church till the close of the seventeenth century, when, the roof and the south aisle falling, the north aisle was fitted up for the use of the parish, with a heavy, short tower. This tower is of the perpendicular order. On its right hand as you face it, stands, in a continued line, the beautiful old western front, in a richly decorated style, with a fine large window from which all the tracery has disappeared. This front is finely ornamented with niches, and statues of saints as large as life; and on the summit formerly were pinnacles, with the figures of St. Bartholomew and St. Guthlac. These have long fallen; but this front, now greatly decayed, and a portion of the south aisle in continuance, show that, in its perfection, Croyland was one of the most beautiful monasteries in the kingdom.

On the weſt ſide of the church ſtands the famous Triangular Bridge, the only one of the kind, I believe, remaining in the kingdom. It was built to admit three ſtreams at their confluence, which ran through the town and met here. It conſiſts of three ſemi-arches uniting in a common centre, and forming,

TRIANGULAR BRIDGE AT CROYLAND.

by their junction, as many pointed arches. It is ſuppoſed to have been deſigned as a ſymbol of the Trinity. It is too ſteep for carriages, and is little uſed even by horſes. There was a bridge here as early as A.D. 943; it being mentioned in King Edward's charter of that date, and again in King Edgar's charter, A.D. 966; but the prefent ftructure is not thought to be older than the reign of Edward I. At the end of the bridge next the London road are the remains of a ftatue, now much mutilated, but defcribed in old books as that of King Ethelbald, the founder of the abbey. It was, when unbroken, in a fitting pofture, dreffed in royal robes, and with a globe in its hand.

The Triangular Bridge poffeffes the additional intereft of being placed at the junction of the three counties of Lincoln, Cambridge, and Northampton.

Castleacre Priory.

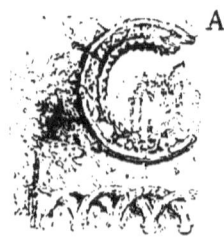ASTLEACRE PRIORY, in Norfolk, is one of the earliest Norman priories in England. It was founded by William de Warrene, the first Earl of Surrey, in 1085, only nineteen years after the Conquest. The remains of the west front, with portions of the north and south transept, show that it was erected in the highest style of Norman architecture. It has scarcely any projecting buttresses, but its level façade is enriched by successive tiers of arch-work, some of these simple, others interlacing. The great western entrance has a very rich round arch of many recesses or mouldings, elaborately ornamented with the zigzag, the dot, and other ornaments. Similar archways give entrance on either hand to the transepts, but they are less ornate, and of smaller dimensions. Within the great round arch is a lesser pointed one, evidently inserted afterwards to contract the passage to a more convenient size. Around and above this great archway are four successive tiers of arches running along the whole face of the front,—the lower and third interlacing, the second short and round, the fourth and uppermost consisting of curious zigzag arches. There has been a noble lofty window over the great western door, apparently of the perpendicular order. Altogether, the western front must have been very beautiful.

The description of the Priory in Blomfield's History, in 1775, shows that the whole of the structure was of equal elegance, and was a place of great extent: " The site of the priory church, which lies west of the castle, was a venerable large Gothic pile of freestone, flint, &c., and built in a cathedral or conventual manner. Great part of the front, or west end of it, is

CASTLEACRE PRIORY: WEST FRONT.

still remaining, where the principal entrance was through a great arch, over which was a stately window. On each side of the great door were doors to enter into the north and south aisles. At the north and south ends of this front stood two towers, supported by strong arches and pillars. The nave, or body, had twelve great pillars, making seven arches on each side, the lowest joining to the towers. On the east end of the nave stood the grand tower, supported by four great pillars, through which was the entrance into the choir. On the south and north sides of this tower were two cross aisles or transepts; and at the end of the north transept there seems to have been a chapel or vestry. The choir was of equal breadth with the nave and aisles, but much shorter, and the east end of it was in form of a chapel. The chapter-house seems to have joined the east side of the cloister, and the dormitory to have been near the west part of the cloister. West of the cloister, and adjoining, was the prior's apartment, now converted into a farm-house. In a large room above-stairs, called the prior's dining-room, is a curious bow-window of stone, consisting of nine panels. In the first were the arms of the priory, painted on glass; in the second, the arms of the Earl of Arundel, and Earl Warren, quarterly, but now broken and gone; in the third, Mowbray, Duke of Norfolk, gules, a lion rampant argent; fourth, the red and white rose united, and a crown over it; fifth, France and England, quarterly; sixth, the rose, &c., as above; seventh, Earl Warren's arms; eighth, quarterly, the Earl of Arundel in the first and fourth quarter, and in the second and third, Maltravers, sable, fretty, or, and Fitz-Alan, Baron of Clun, per fess, azure, and argent quarterly; ninth, argent, a cross componè, or and azure, between twelve cross crosslets, fitchè sable: the priory arms, I take it; and these letters J. W. joined together by a knot, and, under it, SPITV. PRINCIPALI. CONFIRMA. ME. By this it appears that this window was built by John Winchelsey, prior in the reign of Henry VII. or VIII."

Blomfield thinks this was originally a chapel, and part of the original erection, having the arms of Warren conspicuous on its fouth wall, but that it was afterwards altered into a dining-room. He adds, "The fite of this priory took in feveral acres. The grand entrance was north of the priory church, where is now ftanding a large and ftately gatehoufe of free-ftone. Over the arch, as you enter, are the arms of the Earl Warren, of Arundel, and Warren, quarterly, France and England, and thofe of the priory. The whole fite was enclofed with a lofty ftone wall, good part of which is ftill ftanding."

In thefe armorial bearings we have, in fact, a hiftory of the patronage of the priory. In the firft place it was that of the Warrens, Earls of Surrey. Thefe were amongft the moft powerful nobles in England from the Conqueft till the reigns of the Edwards. Warren came over with the Conqueror, and obtained great eftates in Surrey and Norfolk. He is faid to have been fon-in-law to the Conqueror, having married his fifth daughter. We find Earl Warren amongft the very firft noblemen who oppofed the arbitrary acts of King John. He was one of the four who figned the inftructions given by John to Pandulph, engaging to obey the pope; but when John fet at defiance both his engagement to the pope and his engagements to the barons, Warren was one of the three,—namely, Cardinal Langton and the Earls of Pembroke and Warren,—who were fent as a deputation to John at Oxford; and, not obtaining fatisfaction, he was one of the barons who appeared at Runny-mede, and compelled the king to fign Magna Charta. Again, in the thirteenth century, we find the then Earl Warren taking a prominent part in the refiftance of the barons to the encroachments of Henry III., and appearing on the fide of Mortimer, Earl of Leicefter. Warren, however, accepted the profeffions of the king made in the ftatutes of Oxford, in 1258, and afterwards fought on the royal fide. In the following reign, that of Edward I., when that vigorous monarch endeavoured to recover some of the crown lands which the nobles had usurped under weak sovereigns, and sent forth a commission to examine the titles by which some of the great barons held their estates, he met with a sort of resistance in Earl Warren, which made him pause in so dangerous a course. When his commissioners asked Earl Warren to show his titles, the earl drew his sword, and said : " By this instrument do I hold my lands, and by the same I intend to defend them! Our ancestors, coming into this realm with William the Bastard, acquired their possessions by their good swords. William did not make a conquest alone, or for himself solely ; our ancestors were helpers and participants with him." The astounded commissioners had no answer to such an argument ; and Edward found it best to let the great nobles alone, and to prosecute his inquiries into the titles of men who were not so well prepared with steel logic.

In the course of time, by marriage and otherwise, the Warrens became allied to the Dukes of Norfolk, the Earls of Arundel, the families of Maltravers and Fitz-Alan of Clun, as the arms emblazoned in the priory showed. But, besides these, the Bishops of Norwich and the Archbishops of Canterbury were great patrons of Castleacre, and the list of its benefactors, as given by Dugdale, is very long. It received manors, rectories, advowsons, rents, &c., so that at the dissolution its gross revenue amounted to £324 17s. 5½d., and its clear revenue, £306 11s. 4½d. As early as the thirteenth century, the prior was found to hold four hundred and sixty acres of arable land, twenty of pasture, ten of meadow, five watermills, with liberty of fishing in the neighbouring waters. Besides this, he had thirty-six tenants in the town, with a court baron. Though but a cell of Lewes, yet Castleacre had itself subordinate cells : Mindham, or Mendham, in Suffolk; Bromholm, South Reinham, and Slivesholm in Norfolk; a hospital at Rachenesse, in Southacre, for lepers ; and Crabhouse, or Wigenhall priory, in Norfolk, for Austen nuns. Its monks were of the Cliniac order.

No very remarkable event seems to have broken the age-long tranquillity of Castleacre; but there is one curious entry in its records, which shows how prone people have been at all times to convert benefactions into vested rights. "John Plantagenet, Earl Warren, by his deed of May 10th (9 Edw. II.), recites that, whereas his stewards and others his officers in Norfolk had demanded of this priory certain pensions of meats and drinks as their right, because they had been given at first by the monks, out of their free will and respect to the servants of the Earls of Warren, belonging to their manor of Wike in Castleacre, he by this deed quits claim to the same, and charges his officers not to demand or receive it for the future."

The site of this monastery, within its walled precincts, is said to have contained twenty-nine acres, two roods, ten perches. Great dilapidations have taken place in the ruins since the description quoted above was given of them by Blomfield. Parkins, in his History of Norfolk, gives many pages of the gifts of churches, manors, lands, tithes, &c., by men and women of estate, to this priory.

The Church of Castleacre, which formerly belonged to the priory, is a large regular building, in which lie buried, amongst other ancients, the remains of Old Paine, of Castleacre, who was standard-bearer to Henry VIII. A little towards the east of the priory stood the castle of the Earls of Warren and Surrey, on a rising ground, including within its fortifications and outworks about eighteen acres of ground in a circular form. No doubt it was in this strong place that the Earl Warren of

Edward I.'s time received the royal commiffioners, and produced his fword as his title to his eftates. In this caftle the earl received the king, Edward I. himfelf, in 1297; and it appears to have been his favourite refidence, although he had 140 lordfhips in Norfolk befides.

CASTLEACRE PRIORY: INTERIOR.

On the death of John, Earl Warren, in 1347, in the twenty-fixth year of the reign of Edward III., the eftates and title paffed to his nephew, Richard Fitz-Alan, Earl of Arundel, the fon of his fifter Alice, and the title thence became Surrey and Arundel. His fon Richard, Earl of Surrey and Arundel, rendering great fervices to Richard II., received a confiderable grant of money for thefe fervices; yet, in the twenty-firft year of the fame king, he was attainted and beheaded, and his eftates and this manor granted to his fon-in-law, Thomas Mowbray, Earl-Marfhal and Earl of Nottingham, afterwards Duke of Norfolk, who is faid to have been fo inhuman as to bind up his father-in-law's eyes, and become his executioner.

The earldom of Arundel paffed by marriage into the family of the Duke of Norfolk; but Caftleacre was fold by Henry, Earl of Arundel, in the firft year of Queen Elizabeth, to Sir Thomas Grefham, and was conveyed by him to Thomas Cecil, Earl of Exeter. Sir Edward Coke, Lord Chief Juftice, bought Caftleacre of William Cecil, Earl of Exeter, whofe fifter Elizabeth he married; and in this family it remained, Thomas Coke, Earl of Leicefter, dying poffeffed of it in 1759.

Richmond Caftle.

ICHMOND is the capital of the weftern part of the North Riding of Yorkfhire. Camden fays,—"Richmondfhire, or Rich-Mountfhire, from the caftle built there on the Mount, comprehends the five wapentakes of Gilling Weft and Eaft, Hang Weft and Hang Eaft, Halchold, and Claro: bounded on the north by the river Tees; on the eaft by the river Whifk, a branch of the Swale; on the weft by Weftmoreland, and on the fouth by the river Nide and the Weft Riding."

Leland defcribes the country round as at once beautiful and fertile:—"The whole country of Richmontfhire, by eaft from the hills and dales, is plentiful of whete and rye, and metely good meadows and woods. The beft woods lye by eaft of Swale and Ure rivers. In the dales they burn linge, petes and turfes. In places where they cut down linge, good grafs fpringeth for the cattle for a yere or two until the linge overgrow it. There is plenty of good ftone to be quarried in very many places of Richmontfhire. The fhire hath plenty of tyllage. There be no colepits in Richmont; yet the eafterly parts of Richmontfhire burne much fe coles brought out of Durham. There be fome veins of cole found in the upper part of the weſt mounts of Richmont, but not uſed for incommodity of carriage to the lower part."

" Almoſt the whole country," ſays Camden, " riſes in craggy rocks and ridges of hills, among which are graſſy vales; and the bottoms and dales are tolerably fertile. The hills themſelves yield plenty of lead, coal, and copper. For, in the charter of Edward IV., we find a copper mine near the town of Richmond. But avarice, which would urge mankind to carry their reſearches even to hell itſelf, has made no great progreſs in theſe mountains, diſcouraged, perhaps, by the difficulty of carriage."

He notices the abundant limeſtone depoſits and their foſſils: —" As to the ſtones reſembling ſea ſhells and other marine productions, found on the tops of hills, as well as in other places, if they are not *luſus naturæ*, I ſhould ſuppoſe them certain evidences of the univerſal deluge of Noah, agreeable to the opinion of Oroſius, a Chriſtian hiſtorian, who thus expreſſes himſelf:—' When the ſea, under Noah, covered the whole earth, and the deluge overſpread the whole globe, all was air and ſea. We have it on the authority of writers of undoubted veracity, that all mankind was deſtroyed except the few preſerved in the ark, in reward of their faith, to repeople the world. Theſe facts are confirmed even by thoſe who, without knowing the tranſactions of paſt times, or even the Author of time itſelf, have yet been led to conjecture it by evidence and appearances of ſtones which we find in hills remote from the ſea, full of ſhells and oyſters, and frequently hollowed by water.' "

The ſide next to Lancaſhire excites his aſtoniſhment by its wildneſs:—" On the ſide of the country next to Lancaſhire is ſuch a dreary waſte and horrid wilderneſs among the mountains, that certain little rivulets that creep here are called by the neighbourhood 'hell becks;' *q. d.*, rivers or ſtreams of hell, and eſpecially that at the head of the Ure, which runs under a bridge of a ſingle rock in ſo deep a channel as to ſtrike beholders with horror. In this part the goats, deer, and ſtags, of extraordinary ſize, with branching horns, find a ſecure retreat."

The goats, deer, and ſtags have long ſince vaniſhed, but the ſtern ruggedneſs of the ſcenery remains. By following the courſes of the two chief rivers, the Ure and the Swale, Camden informs us of the numerous families of diſtinction which then held the property of the country for the moſt part. Theſe were the Medcalfes of Nappa, " a houſe with towers," who, he ſays, were at that time reckoned the moſt numerous family in all England. "I have heard," he ſays, " that Sir Charles Medcalfe, the firſt of this family, was attended by three hundred perſons of the ſame family, and in the ſame livery, on horſeback, when, as ſheriff of the county, he met the judges and conducted them to York." Sir Charles, he adds, brought crayfiſh from the ſouth of England, and put them into the Ure, which ran paſt his houſe, and forced its way between two rocks at a place thence called Att-Scarre. That the crayfiſh have ever ſince abounded in the Ure, which, quitting Nappa, approached Bolton, the magnificent caſtle of Richard, Lord Scrope, the Chancellor of England. Then leaving the reſidence of the Lords Scrope, it turned eaſtward to the town of Middleham; the honour of which Alan, the firſt Earl of Richmond, who had received it of the Conqueror, conferred on his brother Rinebald, with all the lands which, before their coming, had belonged to Gilpatric the Dane. In the reign of Henry II., Conan, the then Earl of Richmond, likewiſe gave all Wenſleydale to his relative, Robert Fitz-Ralph, who built a very ſtrong tower at Middleham. His great-granddaughter Mary conveyed all this property into the family of the Nevilles by marriage.

The Ure then flows on to Jervaulx, or Jervis, Abbey,— ruined, Camden fays, in his time,— and then to Mafham, poffeffed by a branch of the great family of Scrope of Bolton. On the other fide of the river was Snath, the chief feat of the Lords Latimer, who were defcended from the Nevilles, Earls of Weftmoreland, and which eftate afterwards went by a family of daughters into the families of Percy, Cecil, Danvers, and Cornwallis. The Ure next reached Tanfield, formerly the refidence of the Gernegans, who afterwards merged by marriage into the Greys, Lords of Rotherfield, and affumed the name of Marmion.

The Ure now receives the Swale, which has run from the weftern hills, fcarce five miles above the head of the Ure, and takes the name of the Swale, running by Richmond, and fo to Catterick; or, anciently, Cataracton, from the rapidity of the torrent. The Swale here was famous for Paulinus having baptized in it above ten thoufand Saxons, men, women, and children. In the country around alfo lived the Barons Fitz-Hughs, of Ravenfworth Caftle, defcended from the Saxons, and who had increafed their eftates by marriages with the great families of Marmion and Furneaux, and which then went by marriage to the Fiennes, Lords Dacre of the fouth, and the Parrs.

The Swale, continuing its courfe by Hornby, Bedale, and Topcliffe to Mitton, near Aldborough, then becomes the Oufe, and flows on to York. In this part of its courfe, in Camden's time, it wafhed the eftates of the Fitz-Alans of Bedale, which family merged into thofe of the Stapletons and Greys of Rotherford. At Topcliffe was the chief feat of the Percies.

Here then, following the rivers, we have the catalogue of the chief lords of the foil, the Scropes, Danvers, Marmions, Greys, Percies, Latimers, Nevilles, Fitz-Hughs, and Fitz-Alans, the Furneaux, Fiennes, Dacres, Parrs, &c., all great names in the hiftory of this country during the baronial ages, and moft of them to the time of the Tudors, and fome of them of wealth and diftinction yet. Such was Richmondfhire in Camden's time,—a land of hills and ftreams, of heaths and woods, fair meads and fertile fields; of the chafe, with its deer and ftags of extraordinary fize, and confequently an attractive place to great knights and barons. The centre of this fine wild and yet agricultural country was Richmond, and its caftle was inhabited for many ages by the earls of that name. Thefe were originally earls and then dukes of Brittany. The firft was Alan the Red Earl of Brittany; but it was to his brother Alan the Black that the Conqueror gave Richmondfhire. Conan, the earl in Henry II.'s time, found his earldom of Brittany ufurped by his father-in-law, Vifcount Porheot, and only recovered it by help of Henry II. The fon of Henry, Jeoffrey Plantagenet, married Conftance, the fole heirefs of Conan, and became Earl of Richmond; but the earldom did not defcend in his line, for the fon of Jeoffrey and Conftance, Prince Arthur, was murdered by his uncle, King John of England, and the earldom of Richmond paffed to the iffue of Alice, the only daughter of the Duchefs Conftance, mother of Arthur, by her fecond hufband, Guido, Vifcount of Thouars. The ftory of Prince Arthur has been made immortal by Shakfpeare, and as connected with this caftle and eftate demands a concife recital.

Jeoffrey, the elder brother of John, and father of Arthur, being dead at the time of the death of Richard I., John determined to ufurp from his nephew, a mere boy, not only the throne of England, but the fovereignty of Brittany, Normandy, Touraine, and Anjou. For this purpofe he pretended a will of King Richard's appointing him his succeffor; but, not trufting entirely to this, he collected the barons at Northampton, and there by bribes and fine promifes induced them to elect him as king. The hereditary defcent of the crown had been fo thoroughly broken by the Conqueror, that it was neither then nor for ages after again reftored and firmly fettled. John was playing a defperate game for his pofterity, in making the crown elective, and the gift of the nation. On the other hand, this was a doctrine fo agreeable to the people, that he found no difficulty in procuring the confent of the prelates, and his encrownment by the Archbifhop of Canterbury on this plea. The archbifhop laid it down as a fact that no one could be rightfully monarch in England, except by popular choice and voice; and Matthew of Paris gives thefe words as the opening fpeech of the archbifhop on this occafion: " Hear all ye people! It is well known that no one can have a right to the crown of this kingdon, unlefs for his excellent virtues he be elected to it, and then anointed king, as was the cafe with David, Saul, &c. And thus it was ordained, to the end that he whofe merits are pre-eminent be chofen lord of all the people."

Thereupon the archbifhop declared John the poffeffor of thefe pre-eminent merits, and fo juftly king. The people of Brittany were enthufiaftic in favour of their Prince Arthur; but, unfortunately for him, he had in John of England and Philip of France two of the moft dangerous enemies in the guife of pretended friends. Each was anxious to feize on his territories, and one was as unfcrupulous as the other. Conftance, the mother of Arthur, a woman of ftrong paffions and full of intrigue, had lately married a third hufband, the fecond being ftill alive. She carried her boy to the King of France to infure his fafety againft John, and offered the direct vaffalage of Normandy, Anjou and Aquitaine, which belonged to Arthur, as the price of this protection. Philip, too glad to possess such a pretext for invasion, joined William Desroches, the commander of the Breton force, and took several towns and castles on the frontiers of Brittany from the English; but he soon betrayed his design by destroying these castles, in order to lay open the country to entrance at his pleasure. Desroches, indignant at this proceeding, withdrew Arthur and his mother from the French court. Philip, however, regained the person of Arthur, and promised not only to respect his interests, but to make them his own by marrying him to his daughter Mary. But he was not long in sacrificing all these interests in a peace which he was compelled to make with John; and that ruthless tyrant invaded Aquitaine and Poictou, where he did all he could for a time to ingratiate himself with the nobles, but ended by carrying off Isabella, the daughter of the Count of Angoulême, and the wife of the powerful Count De la Marche, a very beautiful woman. John had been married ten years to Avisa, the daughter of the Earl of Gloucester, a handsome and good woman, notwithstanding which he married Isabella too, at Angoulême; the Archbishop of Bordeaux being pliant enough to perform the ceremony; and John then brought her over to England, and not only paraded her there, but had her crowned, and himself recrowned with her, by the equally pliant Archbishop of Canterbury. In the meantime, the Count De la Marche, in revenge for the abduction of his wife, raised a great rebellion in Poictou and Aquitaine; and in the following year, 1202, the King of France incited Prince Arthur to assert his rights in Aquitaine, and furnished him with 200 knights; promising himself, at the same time, to invade Normandy on his behalf. Arthur was still but a boy of fifteen years of age, his mother was dead, and he was totally incapable of competing with the stout soldiers of John. The Bretons followed him with 500 knights and 4,000 foot-soldiers, and the barons of Touraine and Poictou sent him 110 men-at-arms. Arthur was advised to lay siege to Mirabeau, where his grandmother, Eleanor of Aquitaine, was residing. This violent and licentious woman, who had filled her own house with hatred and rebellion, and had instigated her sons to a most unnatural insurrection against their father, King Henry II., had proved as fierce an enemy to both Arthur and his mother. The town was soon taken, but Eleanor threw herself into the citadel; and before this could be reduced, John was upon the Breton army, and not only secured the person of Arthur, but of 200 knights and nobles; amongst them the Count De la Marche himself, and the Viscounts of Limoges, Lusignan and Thouars, the last being the second husband of Constance, Arthur's mother. John took such a vengeance on these noblemen as was congenial to his diabolic nature: he threw them into dungeons in Normandy and England, where most of them were left to perish of hunger. Of those carried over to England, twenty-two are said thus to have perished in the dungeons of Corfe Castle in Dorsetshire, where, in Saxon times, Edward the Martyr was murdered by his step-mother, Elfrida. There are various traditions of the fate of the unhappy Arthur, but all having a tragical termination. John confined him first in the castle of Falaise, and then in the castle of Rouen, where all positive knowledge of him ceases. Matthew of Paris says that at Falaise John endeavoured to coax the boy to trust to the kindness of his uncle; but that Arthur replied, indignantly, " Give me mine inheritance, restore to me my kingdom of England;" that from that time John determined his death, removed him to Rouen, with orders to keep him closely confined, and that nothing more was ever known of him. It was,

T

however, univerfally reported that John had murdered him with his own hand; and the Monks of Margan entered it in their Yearly Notes that " John, being at Rouen in the week before Eafter, 1203, after he had finifhed his dinner, inftigated by drunkennefs and malignant fiends, literally embrewed his hands in the blood of his defencelefs nephew, and caufed his body to be thrown into the Seine, with heavy ftones faftened to his feet;—that the body was notwithftanding caft on fhore, and burnt at the abbey of Bec, fecretly, for fear of the tyrant."

A popular tradition of the Bretons is that John took Arthur from the caftle of Rouen, and on the way towards Cherbourg, as they travelled on horfeback one evening, having outridden the reft of the company, they paufed on a high cliff over the fea, where John fuddenly thruft the poor boy through with his fword, and toppled him over the precipice, ftill alive and begging for mercy, into the fea. Ralph, the Abbot of Cogges-hall, gives the ftory as moft nearly followed by Shakfpeare. He fays that at Falaife fome of John's courtiers,—and hiftory fhows that he had a number about him as complete fiends as himfelf,—affured him that the Bretons were widely plotting for the refcue of Arthur, advifed that he fhould put out his eyes, and thus render him incapable of governing; that John fent fome hardened villains to execute this atrocity; but that the compaffion of his guards, and efpecially of Hubert de Burgh, the warden of the caftle, prevented this. He was, therefore, removed to Rouen, where John fent for the victim into a boat at night on the river, and there ordered his efquire, Peter de Maulac, to murder him; but that, Maulac fhrinking from the crime, John himfelf, in fpite of the lad's prayers for mercy, ftabbed him and flung him overboard. Hemingford and Knyghton, on the other hand, affert that De Maulac did the deed. At all events he appears to have been an accomplice in it; for John soon after gave him the heirefs of Mulgref in marriage, as the reward for his crime.

This is the tradition which Shakfpeare has followed; but, inftead of Falaife and Rouen, he has placed the fcene of thefe horrid deeds in the caftle of Northampton; and relieved John of the actual murder, by making Arthur kill himfelf by a fall from the caftle wall in endeavouring to efcape. The reader will recollect the mafterly manner in which the poet makes the monfter John impart to Hubert the deadly deed he intends him to execute:—

> *John (to Hubert).* Hubert, I am almoft afhamed
> To fay what good refpect I have of thee.
> *Hubert.* I am much bounden to your Majefty.
> *John.* Good friend, thou haft no caufe to fay fo yet:
> But thou fhalt have; and time creep ne'er fo flow,
> Yet it fhall come for me to do thee good.
> I had a thing to fay,—but let it go:
> The fun is in the heaven, and the proud day,
> Attended with the pleafures of the world,
> Is all too wanton and too full of gawds
> To give me audience. If the midnight bell
> Did, with his iron tongue and brazen mouth,
> Sound one unto the drowfy race of night:
> If this fame were a church-yard where we ftand,
> And thou poffeffed with a thoufand wrongs;
> Or if that furly fpirit, melancholy,
> Had baked thy blood, and made it heavy, thick;
> (Which elfe runs tickling up and down the veins,
> Making that idiot, laughter, keep men's eyes,
> And ftrain their cheeks to idle merriment,
> A paffion hateful to my purpofes;)
> Or if that thou couldft fee me without eyes,
> Hear me without thine ears, and make reply
> Without a tongue, ufing conceit alone
> Without eyes, ears, and harmful found of words,
> Then, in defpite of brooded watchful day,
> I would into thy bofom pour my thoughts:
> But ah, I will not:—yet I love thee well.

The monfter king, however, does unfold his defign, and Hubert pretends to execute it, but does not. After Arthur's death, Philip of France, on pretext of avenging Arthur, invaded the British possessions in that kingdom; and, in 1205, Normandy, Anjou, Maine, Touraine, and Poictou, successively fell into his hands, and were lost to the English crown, and became the cause of long subsequent wars. Thus John paid dearly for his treason to his nephew: nor did his troubles end here: his whole life was one great trouble. His barons revolted; Lewis, the Dauphin of France, invaded England at their invitation, and this country had a narrow escape of becoming a French province. Such are the romantic incidents of the short life of one of the earliest earls of Richmond.

After the death of Arthur, Guido, Viscount de Thouars, the second husband of Constance, became Earl of Richmond; then Ranulph III., Earl of Chester, her third husband. To him succeeded Peter de Dreux, who married the only daughter of Alice, only daughter of Constance, by Guido de Thouars. In this line it descended till the reign of Edward III., several of the earls marrying into the royal family. Edward III. gave the earldom for a time to his son, John of Gaunt; and subsequently to John de Montfort, Duke of Brittany. In Richard II.'s reign he lost this earldom by taking part with France; and the king gave it to Montfort's sister Joan, widow of Ralph Basset, of Draiton. It then passed to Ralph Neville, Earl of Westmoreland; after him to John, Duke of Bedford. Henry VI. conferred it on his own brother, Edward de Hadham, by particular right, that he might have a seat next to the dukes in parliament; and thus it came to his son, Henry VII. of England. Before Henry won the crown, and while he lived in exile, the earldom was possessed by the brothers of Edward IV.—the Duke of Clarence who perished in the butt of sack; and Richard, Duke of Gloucester, the usurper. Henry VIII. conferred the earldom on a natural son of his, who died without children.

James I. presented the earldom of Richmond to Henry Lodowic, Duke of Lennox, whom he created Duke of Richmond. In that line it continued till 1672, when, on its lapse, Charles I. conferred the dukedom on his natural son by Louisa Querouaille, Duchess of Portsmouth, whom he created Duke of Lennox, Earl of Darnley, Baron Methuen of Torbolton, in Scotland, and Duke of Aubigne, in France. In this family the title and estates still remain.

Thus it appears that Richmond Castle has, since its first erection, been successively in possession of families closely connected with royalty; often reverting to the crown, to be again conferred on some allied person, and frequently on the natural children of the monarch. It has in turn been in the hands of every different dynasty. Plantagenet, York, Lancaster, Tudor, and Stuart, all have been its masters, and its bestowers. Mad King John, John of Gaunt, "hump-backed Richard," Henry VII., all were lords of Richmond. If it has produced no one of particular pre-eminence of genius, it has been the property of those who have made a tolerable noise in the world; but no part of its history is so interesting as its connection with the unfortunate Prince Arthur. Its union for so many generations with the dukedoms of Brittany and Normandy gives it also a greater historical importance: that the dukes of Brittany, the princes of Aquitaine, Touraine, Normandy, and Poictou, should also have their house, estate, and title in this Yorkshire district, seems now-a-days curious.

But long before the days of the Bretons and Normans, this neighbourhood was a favourite place with the Romans. Numerous coins of various Roman emperors have been dug up on the castle hill; and the foundations of Roman stations, with coins, urns, and other relics, have been found at Catteric, and still more at Bowes and on the banks of the Greta; with altars and memorial ſtones, the inſcriptions on ſome of which will be found in Leland and Camden. Leland's account of Richmond itſelf is quaint: " Richmond town is waullid, and the caſtle on the river ſide of Swale is as the knot of the cumpace of the waulle. In the waulle be three gates: French

RICHMOND CASTLE.

gate, the moſt occupied in the north part of the town ; Finkel-ſtreete-gate, Bargate ; al three be down ; veſtiges yet remain. In the market-place is a large chapel of the Trinite. The cumpace of the ruinous waulles is not half a mile about. There are ſuburbs to all the gates ; but French-gate ſuburb is almoſt as big as the other ſuburbs, and in it is the pariſh church of the whole town. At the back of the French gate is the Grey Freres, a little without the walls, so that the town walle compassith litle but the market-place, the howses about it, and the gardens between them. The castle is nere hand, much in cumpace as the circuit of the town wall, but now it is in mere ruin. There is a conduit of water, elfe there is none in Richmond.

"I cam through the great long strete in Richmont, or I cam to the top of the hill where the best of the town called the bailly and the castle; some think that the place where the baily is was once *externa area castelli*, and since builded with houses. Waulled it was, but the waull is now decayed. The names and places of four or five gates remain. There is a chapel in Richmond town, with strange figures in the walls of it. The people there deeme that it was once a temple of idols."

Camden in his time describes the monastery of the Grey Friars in Richmond as reduced to its beautiful square tower, and says:—"The castle stands upon the south side of the hill, overhanging the river, with a large cataract just under it. A more inaccessible situation can hardly be conceived. The site is circular. On the north it was defended by a deep ditch and drawbridge, whose arch, buried by time, was discovered in 1732 by the industry of Mr. Wharton, agent to the Duke of Richmond; but it has since been buried, and a house been built on or near it. The prodigious rise of the ground conceals the entrance to the castle, the spacious arch of which may be seen within, stopped up under or near a square tower, ninety-nine feet high, of three stories, built by Conan, Earl of Richmond, in the twelfth century, with a large round column in the middle, which once supported the flooring. From its top is a most extensive prospect over Swaledale, a deep valley with rich pasture, between a chain of bleak, dreary hills, extending north to Stanemore, and west to Westmoreland. On the south side of the area was the chapel and hall. In the east wall, which is most entire, are two towers, called Robin Hood's and the Golden Tower."

There was a Priory of St. Martin at Richmond, which was a cell to the abbey of St. Mary at York. It was founded by Wymar, dapifer or steward to the Earl of Richmond, about the year 1100, with certain lands in its neighbourhood; and a cell of nine or ten monks sent from St. Mary's at York was settled there, and continued till the dissolution.

Let us now see how Richmond and its castle look at the present day. A recent writer (Walter White) shows them to us with the old features still looking through sundry modern ones:—" You come to the brow of a long declivity, the end of the moors, and are rewarded by a view which rivals that seen from Scarthe Nick. Swaledale opens before you, overspread with waving fields of grain, with numerous farmsteads scattered up and down, with a long range of cliff breaking the opposite slope, and, about four miles distant, Richmond, its lofty seat crowned by the square castle keep, tall and massive. I saw it lit by the afternoon sun, and needed no better invitation for a half-hour's halt on the heathery bank. You descend to the wheat-fields, and see no more of the town till close upon it. Swale, as you will notice while crossing the bridge, still shows the characteristics of a mountain stream. Very steep is the grass-grown street leading from the river up to the main part of the town. The castle occupies the summit of a bluff, which, rising bold and high from the Swale, commands a noble prospect over what Whitaker calls 'the Piedmont of Richmondshire.' On the other side, towards the river, the walls are all broken and ruinous, with here and there a loophole, or window opening, through which you may look abroad on the landscape, and ponder on the changes which have befallen since Alan the Red built a fortress here on the lands given to him in reward for prowess by the Conqueror. It was in 1071 that he began to fortify, and portions of his masonry yet remain, fringed with ivy and tufts of grass, and here and there the bugloss growing from the crevices. Perhaps, while you saunter to and fro in the castle-yard, the keeper will appear, and tell you—though not without leave—his story of the ruins. If it will add to your pleasure, he will show you the spot where George IV. sat when Prince of Wales, and declared the prospect to be the finest he had ever beheld. You will be told which is Robin Hood's Tower, which the Gold Tower,—so called because of a tradition that treasure was once discovered therein—and which is Scotland's Hall, where knights, and nobles, and high-born dames held their banquets. And here you will be reminded of Fitzhughs and Marmions, Randolph de Glanville, and William the Lion, of Nevilles and Scropes, and of the Lennox—a natural son of Charles II.—to whom the Merry Monarch gave the dukedom of Richmond, and to whose descendants it still belongs.

"One side of the garth is enclosed by a new building, to be used as barracks or a military depot, and near this, at the angle towards the town, rises the keep. What a mighty tower it is! ninety-nine feet high, the walls eleven feet thick, strengthened on all sides by straight buttresses, an impressive memorial of the Normans. It was built by Earl Conan, seventy-five years after Alan the Red's bastions. The lowest chamber is dark and vaulted, with the rings still remaining to which the lamps were hung, and a floor of natural rock pierced by the old well. The chief entrance is now on the first floor, to which you mount by an outer stair, and the first things you see on entering are the arms and accoutrements of the Yorkshire Militia, all carefully arranged. The view from the top delights your eye by its variety and extent—a great scene of green hills and woods, the winding dale, and, beyond, the brown heights that stretch away to the mountains. You see the town and all its picturesque features; the towers of St. Mary's and the old Gray Friars' Monastery, and Trinity Chapel at the side of the Market-place, now desecrated by an intrusion of petty merchandize. And, following the course of the river downwards, you can see in the meadows among the woods the ruins of the Abbey of St. Agatha, at Easby. A few miles further, and the stream flows past Catterick, the Cattaractonium of the Romans, and Bolton-on-Swale, the burial-place of Old Jenkins.

"On leaving the castle, make your way down the path which runs round the face of the precipice below the walls, yet high enough above the river for pleasing views; a good place for an evening stroll. Then descend to a lower level, and look back from the new bridge, near the railway station; you will be charmed with the singularly picturesque view of the town, clustered all along the hill-top, and terminated by the imposing mass of ruins, and the lordly keep. And there is something to be seen near at hand; the station, built in Gothic style, pleasantly situated amongst the trees; St. Martin's Cell, founded more than seven hundred years ago, now sadly dilapidated, and used as a cow-stall. Beyond, on the slope of the hill, stands the parish church, with a fine lofty tower; and near it are the old grammar-school, famous for good scholars; and the Tate Testimonial, a handsome Gothic edifice, with cloisters, where the boys play in rainy weather. It was in that churchyard that Herbert Knowles wrote the poem,—

<blockquote>Methinks it is good to be here,</blockquote>

which has long kept his name in memory."

From this Castle-hill you have pleasant views of gardens and meadows below; of Easby Abbey, amid its noble trees, near the river, which was, for centuries, the burial-place of the Scropes, who became possessors of Easby not long after the death of Roald, constable of Richmond, founder of the abbey, in 1152. In the meadow beyond you also see the gate-house mantled with ivy, and Easby's pretty little church between the gate-house and the ruins of the abbey. But, without wandering farther, we may with Walter White " take another stroll" on the path under the castle, thinking of the ancient legend, and wishing for a peep at the mysterious vault where King Arthur's warriors lie asleep. Long, long ago, a man, while wandering about the hill, was conducted into an underground vault by a mysterious personage, and there he saw to his amazement a great multitude lying in slumber. Ere he recovered, his guide placed in his hands a horn and a sword. He drew the blade half out of the sheath, when lo! every sleeper stirred as if about to awake, and the poor mortal, terror-stricken, loosed his hold; the sword slid back, and the opportunity for release was lost, to recur no more for many a long day. The unlucky wight heard as he crept forth a bitter voice crying:—

> Potter, Potter Thompson!
> If thou had either drawn
>   The sword, or blown that horn,
> Thoud'st been the luckiest man
>   That ever was born.

With its history and its legends, and its beautiful situation and fine surrounding country, Richmond Castle stands a distinguished ruin amongst the brave old remains of the feudal days of England; and what a healthy place it must be! That reference to " Old Jenkins " is full of moment in the history of longevity; for he was but one of a number of men who, in his time (the reigns of Henry VIII., Edward VI., Mary, and

Elizabeth) lived beyond their hundred years, in that neighbourhood; and, long as is this article, we ought not to close it without the fitting testimony to its healthiness by a short notice of Old Jenkins and his old associates. We have the following account of these living antiquities by Mrs. Anne Saville, who lived at Bolton-on-Swale in the reign of Elizabeth:—

"When I came to live at Bolton, I was told several particulars of the great age of Henry Jenkins; but I believed little of the story for many years, till one day, he coming to beg an alms, I desired him to tell me truly how old he was. He paused a little, and then said, that to the best of his remembrance he was about 162 or 163; and I asked what kings he remembered. He said Henry VIII. I asked what public thing he could longest remember. He said, Flodden Field. I asked whether the king was there. He said, No: he was in France, and the Earl of Surrey was general. I asked him how old he might be then. He said, 'I believe I might be between ten and twelve; for,' said he, 'I was sent to Northallerton with a horse-load of arrows, but they sent a bigger boy from thence to the army with them.' All this agreed with the history of that time; for bows and arrows were then used; the earl he named was general; and King Henry VIII. was then at Tournay. And yet it is observable that this Jenkins could neither read nor write. There were also four or five in the same parish that were reputed all of them to be a hundred years old, or within two or three years of it, and they all said he was an elderly man ever since they knew him; for he was born in another parish, and before any registers were in churches, as it is said. He told me then, too, that he was butler to the Lord Conyers, and remembered the abbot of Fountains Abbey very well before the dissolution of the monasteries.

"Henry Jenkins departed this life, December 8, 1670, at

Ellerton-upon-Swale, in Yorkshire. The Battle of Flodden Field was fought September 9, 1513, and he was twelve years old when Flodden Field was fought; so that this Henry Jenkins lived 169 years; viz., sixteen years longer than Old Parr, and was, it is supposed, the oldest man born upon the ruins of the postdiluvian world.

"In the last century of his life he was a fisherman, and used to trade in the streams; his diet was coarse and sour, and towards the latter end of his days he begged up and down. He has sworn in Chancery and other courts to above 140 years' memory, and was often at the assizes at York, whither he generally went on foot; and I have heard some of the country gentlemen affirm that he frequently swam in the rivers after he was past the age of a hundred years. In the King's Remembrancer's Office, in the Exchequer, is a record of a deposition in a cause by English bill between Anthony Clarke and Smirkson, taken in 1665, at Kettering in Yorkshire, where Henry Jenkins, of Ellerton-upon-Swale, labourer, aged 157 years, was produced, and deposed as a witness. About seventy years after his death, a monument was erected at Bolton, by a subscription of the parishioners, to perpetuate the memory of this remarkable man. Upon it was engraved this inscription: —'Blush not, marble, to rescue from oblivion the memory of Henry Jenkins, a person of obscure birth, but of a life truly memorable; for he was enriched with the goods of nature, if not of fortune, and happy in the duration, if not variety of his enjoyments; and though the partial world despised and disregarded his low and humble state, the equal eye of Providence beheld and blessed it with a patriarch's health and length of days, to teach mistaken man these blessings are entailed on temperance, a life of labour, and a mind at ease. He lived to the amazing age of 169. Was interred here December 16th, 1670, and had this justice done to his memory, 1743.'"

Camden has fallen into an error regarding Jenkins, making him a refident of the neighbourhood of Bolton Caftle in Uredale, inftead of Bolton-on-Swale. The fact is ftated in the above notice of him; that he lived and died at Ellerton, which is near Bolton-on-Swale, and was buried at this Bolton. Jenkins is faid in this account to have remembered the abbot of Fountains. He had good reafon; for it is ftated that when he ufed to be fent to that great abbey on meffages by Lord Conyers, the abbot always gave him, " befides waffail, a quarter of a yard of roaft-beef for his dinner, and a great black-jack of ftrong beer." He is faid, too, to have fhared the dole of the monks of Jervaux to poor travellers, and therefore had feen that fplendid monaftery in all its glory.

In concluding our notice of Richmond Caftle, it ought not to be omitted that the whole country round is as full of historical reminifcences as it is of natural beauty. In Coverdale was born the venerable reformer of that name, who, with Tyndall and others, produced our earlieft complete edition of the Bible. At Bolton Abbey, Mary Queen of Scots was at one time confined. There, too, lived thofe bold Scropes, one of whom was Chancellor to Richard II., another fought ftoutly at Flodden Field, and a third of whom joined the Pilgrimage of Grace on the diffolution of religious houfes. Of the Lords Scrope of Mafham, one was at the battle of the Standard, and another beheaded for confpiring againft Henry V. Then there is that grand old ruin of Middleham, the feat of the Nevilles, and one of the many caftles of Warwick the King-maker, and where he confined Edward IV. after he had furprifed him in his camp at Wolvey. There, configning him to the fafe cuftody of his brother, the Archbifhop of York, that prelate, unfit cuftodian of fo flippery a fubject, fuffered him to hunt in the park, and fo found that Edward had ridden off, and foon appeared in London. Subtly did Warwick lay his nets to re-catch him, the Archbifhop of York inviting Edward, and Clarence, his brother, to fupper at his manor of Moor in Hertfordfhire, when, juft as the king was wafhing his hands before fitting down to table, fome one whifpered in his ear that an armed band was lying in wait for him near the houfe. Once more Edward got fecretly to horfe, galloped through the night to Windfor, and after many an adventure, and a flight abroad, lived to flay the great king-maker at the battle of Barnet, and break up his overgrown power for ever. In this fame Middleham was born Edward, the only fon of Richard III. And there is Topcliffe, too, juft on the border of Richmond-fhire, where the Earl of Northumberland was lying in bed when the rumour came that his enemies were about to feize him for his intended fhare in the rifing of the North in Elizabeth's time; and he rofe haftily and joined the Earl of Weftmoreland to become in reality a fugitive in Scotland, and to fee England again only as a betrayed gueft, betrayed by the Douglas, and then led to the block. But the whole land is fown with ftirring events, and we can only fay further that Richmond Caftle ftands like a fine hiftoric picture, fet in a fitting frame of great and golden memories.

Byland Abbey.

IN a pleasant valley near Coxwold, in the Wolds of Yorkshire, stands the ruined but still beautiful Abbey of Byland. The style of the remains is peculiar, but extremely light and graceful. These consist of the west front, and one end of the transept. Every part of these remains bears testimony to erection at different periods. The central door has a richly cuspated arch, with several receding pillars and mouldings. Above it is a row of light lancet arches, with a line of similar semi-arches running above them. Higher still is the lower half of a noble circular window. On one side of this main structure remain a heavy round-headed doorway, and a round-headed window above it, both consisting of several pillars and mouldings, evidently of the oldest date in the building. On the left hand is a richly-wrought lancet-headed doorway, and this is all that now remains: sufficient, however, to denote that the monastery, when perfect, was extremely elegant. The date assigned to its first erection accords with the older, round-arched portion, being of the period when the remains of Saxon had not yet disappeared from Norman buildings.

Byland is said to have been founded by Roger de Mowbray, a minor in the wardship of King Stephen, at the suggestion of his mother, Gundreda de Mowbray. The history of the founding was preferved by Philip, the third abbot. The occafion for the erection of Byland Abbey was to eftablifh twelve monks and Gerold their abbot, who had been obliged to flee from Furnefs Abbey, in Lancafhire, by the incurfions of the Scots. They had gone firft to York, where they were hofpitably received by Archbifhop Thurftan, who recommended them to Roger de Mowbray. Gundreda, the mother of Roger, and the widow of Nigil de Albine, entertained them for fome time at the caftle of Threfk, and then fent them to join Robert de Alneto, her near relative, a Norman, living as hermit at Hode, where fhe fupplied them with provifions. Finding, however, that the tranfmiffion of thefe provifions became very inconvenient, fhe requefted her fon to give them his vaccary, or compafture, at Combe, and all the land at Wildon, Seakeldon, and Ergham, for their fupport. Whilft there, the abbot went to Savigny, in Normandy, to procure exemption from their former fubjection to Furnefs, which was done by a general chapter of the order; and the abbot returned to York, where he died, and was buried at Hode. In his place, Roger, the fub-cellarar, one of the monks who left Furnefs, was made abbot. The brethren remained at Hode till A.D. 1143, when they found the fpot unfuitable for the founding of a monaftery, and at the requeft of their patronefs, Gundreda, Roger de Mowbray, her fon, gave them the church and town of Biland, or Bella-landa-fuper-Moram, near the river Rye, and nearly oppofite to the Abbey of Rievaux. This would have been a charming fituation, but, being within found of each other's bells, it did not agree with their notions of monaftic feclufion, and they again removed to Stocking, near Coxwold, under Blakhow Hill. At this place they repaired an old church, and built a cloifter and other houfes; and now they feemed to have found a permanent abode. They continued there for thirty years, but these were by no means years of peace and uninterrupted religious contemplation. The abbots of Calder and Furness, notwithstanding the exemption which they had obtained from their jurisdiction, commenced law proceedings to compel them again to submission. These vexatious proceedings were not brought to a close till the year 1155, the first year of the reign of Henry II. They were then determined in their favour by the abbot of Rievaux, who had been appointed judge, and the Archbishop of York took them under his direct protection.

Being now at ease, the monks selected a yet more eligible site for their monastery, and finally raised it in a valley a little more to the eastward, having drained the marshes and cleared a large tract of woodland. The abbey, of which we now have the remains, was completed and entered upon A. D. 1177, 23 Hen. II. It stood near to Burtoft and Berfclive, between Whitaker and Cambe Hill, a pleasant and retired situation. It was dedicated to the Virgin Mary, and continued to flourish till the dissolution.

Byland was not one of the abbeys which ever raised itself into princely state amongst the monasteries of England. It was not one of the mitred establishments, whose heads assumed the state of nobles, and attended parliaments with the retinue of princes; but it had many privileges, and was a well-to-do and independent community. The Biland which the monks had left near Rievaux was thenceforth known as Old Byland: this new Byland was distant about five miles from Rievaux; and after crossing a moor, as you descended a very steep hill, the prospect of a very fine country opened upon you, with this abbey and the village near it. Henry II., Henry III., and Henry VI. granted especial privileges to Byland. It was exempted from all tolls, pontage, &c., from paying any sort of gelds, scutage, or hidage, from performing any duties of the county, wapentake, or riding, and from all aids and fecular fervice. The monks were free in all cities, boroughs, markets, fairs, bridges, and ports, in England and Normandy, and had liberty of holding courts of their own, with fac, foc, thal, theam, infangentheof, and utfangentheof. They could be fued by no magiftrate except the king or his chief juftice. They had free warren over all their demefnes, and no perfon could intrude upon them. Henry III. made them free of ward-penny, over-penny, thething-penny, hengwith, flemwith, blodewite, leirwith, flemefrith, grithbreth, foreftal, hamfokne, heinfare, and all fervice and fecular exactions. He extended their right of trying caufes to their manors of Sutton and Clifton, in Yorkfhire, and at their manor of Wardcope, in Weftmoreland; and Henry VI. gave them a grant of all waifs, ftrays, and forfeiture of felons within their lands. Dugdale gives a long lift of their poffeffions in different places. At the diffolution, the grofs revenue of the abbey was £295 5s. 4d.; the clear income, £238 9s. 4d. It was a profperous abbey of an unambitious kind. No great events are recorded in its annals, nor does it feem to have produced, or had the prefence of, any men of pre-eminently diftinguifhed talents; but one may, from its fubftance and its pleafant fituation, fairly fuppofe it a favoured fpecimen of monaftic retreat.

The vifitor to Byland will not fail to afcend the hill and take a glance at Coxwold, the church and parfonage of Lawrence Sterne. There he will find the fame pulpit in the church in which Sterne preached; and on the right hand fide of the road—the laft houfe, I think, on that fide, on the way towards Byland, — he will fee the fame houfe which Sterne inhabited. There is a parfonage now adjoining the churchyard; but, at this little houfe of two fmall rooms in front, and of two ftories high, the humourift lived. The landlady of the village inn was fond of

BYLAND ABBEY.

talking of Sterne. "A very clever man," she said; "a very clever man, indeed; but he had a daughter much cleverer than himself." "Really," I said; "in what way did she display this extraordinary ability?" "In an extraordinary way," responded the landlady; "by riding about the village on her father's horse with her face to the tail." This, of course, she explained, was when she was a girl of eleven or twelve; but the good woman was not by any means jesting. This feat of equestrianism was in her eyes an exhibition of talent far greater than her father's. What her idea of literary fame was we may imagine.

She assured us, also, that the village doctor lived at Sterne's old house—" a very civil man, a very civil man, indeed; and she was sure he would have much pleasure in showing it to us." Accordingly my friend, who on that occasion was driving me in his carriage to Rievaux Abbey, drew up at the door. I knocked, and was admitted by a maid, who assured me that her master was at home, and would see me in a minute. Whereupon she showed me into a small front room, in which Sterne is said to have written, and there I waited some time. Anon the servant returned, and said her master was coming directly. A while after she returned once more, and asked my name. I gave her my card, and added that I was sorry to trouble her master, as my object was merely to see Sterne's abode; and again she made her appearance to say that her master was engaged and could not see me. The village Galen had discovered that I was not a hoped-for patient, and "the very civil man,—very civil man, indeed," was not civil enough to gratify the curiosity of a stranger by allowing him to see a cottage in which there was literally nothing worth seeing. However, I had been in Sterne's house, and discovered that all his endeavours to inculcate benevolence of sentiment had not penetrated very deep into the nature of his successor, so I adjourned to the church. The sexton attended with the key, and I entered. It is a lofty, plain church, and there stood the old pulpit in which the author of " Tristram Shandy" used to preach. What, however, particularly attracted my attention was a solitary swallow which was flitting about, and giving an occasional twitter as it sought a way out. I looked round; all the windows were closed; there was no way for it to escape, and I immediately thought of Sterne's starling, which was always plaintively crying " I can't get out."

The sexton said it had, no doubt, flown in on Sunday, when

the windows were open, so that it must then (the middle of the week) have been flitting about and vainly seeking egress for several days. "Good man," said I, "pull open one or two of your windows, and let it escape, for Heaven's sake!" And what was the man's cool answer? "Oh, it will die of itself, if we let it alone."

And that was in Sterne's church, in the very front of his pulpit, not many yards from the place where he probably penned that very pathetic incident of the starling, with its cry, so full of pitiful appeal, "I can't get out! I can't get out!" Such is the effect of the finest touches of genius, of the happiest incentives to humanity. Who could have believed that such an incident could possibly have happened where Sterne had penned those words which have thrilled so many a youthful bosom, never again to be forgotten? The sexton had only to pull a cord to open a window high aloft, no doubt the one through which the swallow had entered; but he was reluctant to do it, because, he said, it would let others in; and though he did it at my earnest insistance, I had a feeling that the moment my back was turned he would close it again, without giving the bird time to find its way out. I afterwards felt much vexed with myself that I did not go to the parsonage and ask the clergyman to see that the sexton did let the poor creature "get out."

As we returned through the village on the following day, the Medicus was leaning over his gate as we passed. He was a man of middle age, with a vulgar air, and confiderable quantity of whisker about his face; and he had evidently taken a peep at us the day before, and recognised us as the persons who would have liked to see Sterne's house; for he grinned broadly, and evidently with much self-gratulation, as we drove by, evidently thinking he had done a very clever thing in doing a discourtesy.

Such were the revelations of the tone of mind and the scale of enlightenment in the place where Sterne drew the picture of Uncle Toby and Corporal Trim, where he taught us to respect human sorrows in Lieutenant Le Fevre, the blight of the heart in poor Maria, and the sufferings of animals in the captive starling. As a prophet has no honour in his own country, in that country his teachings are, of course, usually thrown away. Here, instead of feeling, there seemed an utter want of it; instead of the kindliness of Uncle Toby and Corporal Trim, churlish rudeness prevailed, and the highest idea of cleverness was that of a romping girl riding with her face to a horse's tail!

The monastery of Fors, in Yorkshire, was subject to Byland.

Jedburgh Abbey.

HE abbey of Jedburgh was raifed by David I. of Scotland, that founder of fo many religious houfes, in a very pleafant and picturefque, but very dangerous neighbourhood. It was always expofed to the inroads of the hoftile Englifh, and fuffered, as it was fure to do, frequently and grievoufly at their hands. It ftood on the river Jed, near the junction of the Teviot with that river. The ballad of the "Hermit of Warkworth" well pictures the fcenes that were for ages continually occurring in the fair border-lands of England and Scotland.

> Lord Percy and his barons bold
> They fix upon a day,
> To fcour the marches late oppreffed,
> And Scottifh wrongs repay.
>
> The knights affembled on the hills,
> A thoufand horfe and more:
> Brave Widdrington, then funk in years,
> The Percy ftandard bore.
>
> Tweed's limpid current foon they pafs,
> And range the Borders round,
> Down the green flopes of Teviotdale
> Their bugle-horns refound.

And soon turned out to meet them the stout Scottish Borderers; on this ground, as the ballad of " Chevy Chafe " has it,

> All men of pleafant Tivydale,
> Faft by the river Tweed.

A very pleafant dale was Teviotdale, but rather a trying place to live in whilft thefe fifticuff days remained. " The vicinage of this abbey," fays Grofe, " to the Borders, fubjected it to the depredations of every incurfion or invafion. Thefe were, in general, carried on with the greateft cruelty imaginable; neither age, fex, nor profeffion affording the leaft protection, the victors marking their footfteps with fire and fword.

" The ravages committed in the different incurfions of the Englifh had fo damaged this houfe, and reduced its income, as to render it infufficient for the lodging and maintenance of the canons. King Edward I. therefore fent feveral of them to different religious houfes of the fame order in England, there to be maintained till this houfe could be repaired and reftored to better circumftances. One of the writs is ftill extant by which a canon, named Ingelram de Colonia, was fent to the convent of Bridlington, in Yorkfhire."

The abbey of Jedburgh had two cells, one at Reftenote, in Angusfhire, and the other at Canonby, fituated on the river Efke, in Efkedale, in Roxburghfhire; if poffible, a more unlucky fituation than that of Jedburgh. It was frequently plundered and burned by the Englifh, and the prior and canons obliged to flee during the heat of the war, by which means their records were fo often deftroyed, that an accurate account of them is impoffible. The firft monks, who were canons regular, were brought to Jedburgh by David I., from the abbey of St.

Quintin's, at Beauvais, in France. Notwithstanding all the ravages of the Border wars, at the diffolution the revenue of the abbey, with that of its two cells at Restenote and Canonby, amounted to £1274 10s.

The abbey was erected into a temporal lordship in favour of Sir Andrew Kerr of Fernihurst, anceftor to the Marquis of Lothian, who was in high favour with James VI., who made him a peer, with the title of Lord Jedburgh. The abbey and eftate yet remain the property of the Marquis of Lothian. The ruins of the abbey are ftill very fine, and fhow what the building muft have been before it was fo frequently battered and burned by the Englifh invaders. Befides the attacks of Edward I. and Edward III., the Earl of Surrey, in 1523, ftormed and burned Jedburgh, and along with it the abbey. In his difpatch to Henry VIII., he particularly notices the ftout refiftance of the abbey, which, he fays, held them till " twoo houres within night," but does not fpecify when the attack on the abbey commenced. Notwithftanding, one author after another has ftated that the ftorming of the abbey lafted " two hours ;" an evident miftake, founded on the Earl of Surrey's phrafe that it lafted to within two hours of the night.

In this fame difpatch he informs us that " the towne was much better than I weened it had been, for there was twoo tymes moo houfes therein then in Berwicke, and well buylded with many honeft and fair houfes therein, fufficiente to have lodged M horfemen in garnyfon, and fix good towres therein ; which towne and towres be clenely deftroyed, burnt, and throwen downe. Undoubtedly there was noo journey made into Scotlande, in noo mann's day levying, with foo few a nombre, that is recownted to be foo high an enterprife as this, both with thies contremen and Scottifhmen, nor of truthe fo much hurt doon."

This would seem a sufficient destruction for some time; but afterwards the Earl of Hertford committed as great ravages there; and so completely was the place spoiled, that the abbey, in common with the other monasteries in Teviotdale, had ceased to be inhabited at the dissolution. Nor was it from the English alone that these ill-fated Borders received such treatment. The men of Teviotdale were famous for their martial propensities, and were as ready to make raids and plunderings as their enemies, and, therefore, the less to be pitied. " As for the humours of the people of Teviotdale," says Scott of Harden, in the Macfarlane MSS., " they were both strong and warlike, as being inured to war and daily incursions; and the most part of the heritors of the country gave out their lands to their tenants for military attendance, upon rentals, and reserved only some few mainses for their own sustenance, which were laboured by their servants besides their service. They paid an entry, a herauld, and a small rent-duty; for there were no rents raised here that were considerable till King James went into England; yea, all along the Border."

This gives a dismal picture of the state of the border-country till the union of the two kingdoms under one crown. Alternate invasions, burnings, massacres, and every kind of desolation; so that none but men fond of war could live in it, and no profit could be derived from the lands except what consisted in mere defence against invaders. These men, especially those of Jedburgh, fought with axes, which were called Jeddart axes, or Jeddart staves. Scott, in his " Lay of the Last Minstrel," describes the warriors of Branksome Hall, as

<blockquote>With Jedwood axe at saddle-bow.</blockquote>

He says, in his introduction to the " Border Minstrelsy," that, upon the arrival of the ill-fated Mary in her native country, she found the Borderers in a state of great disorder. The exertions of her natural brother, afterwards the famous Regent Murray, were necessary to restore some degree of tranquillity. He marched to Jedburgh, executed twenty or thirty of the transgressors, burnt many houses, and brought a number of prisoners to Edinburgh. No doubt, on these occasions, the military commanders, come from which side they would, retorted on the Jedburgh men what was popularly called "Jeddard justice," hanging them first and trying them after. The unfortunate Queen Mary, finding that the severities of her brother, the Regent, had not quelled the fierce spirit of the Borderers, appointed the Earl of Bothwell commissioner for that purpose; but his unprincipled and licentious conduct only embroiled that wretched district worse. On this, she herself advanced to the Border, determining to hold a court at Jedburgh for the settlement of the peace and the punishment of the offenders; but, hearing that Bothwell was severely wounded in attempting to seize John Elliott of the Parke, a notorious freebooter, in an evil hour for her reputation and happiness, she mounted her horse, and rode to Hermitage Castle (where Bothwell lay) by a circuitous route, and returned the same day, a distance, altogether, of nearly fifty miles. A dangerous morass, still called the Queen's Mire, is pointed out on the way, where she had a narrow escape for her life. On her return to Jedburgh she was seized with a dangerous fever, and lay ill for several weeks at an old mansion still pointed out in the town, and where for some time her death was expected.

The confusion upon the Borders became more and more lawless; and when the rising of the North took place, and the Earls of Northumberland and Westmoreland fled into Scotland, Northumberland was betrayed by Douglas into the hands of Murray the Regent, but Westmoreland was received by the

Laird of Fernichurst, close to Jedburgh, and many of the Teviotdale men were greatly scandalized that the Lords Ferniehurst and Hume had not forcibly rescued Northumberland from the Regent. Murray marched towards Jedburgh to seize Westmoreland and his followers at Ferniehurst; but, as he approached Jedburgh, his men, who had no fancy for the work, nearly all deserted him, and he was obliged to return. In fact, the gentry of the Border, the Humes, Granges, Buccleuchs, Ferniehursts, Johnstones, Armstrongs, Maxwells, Kerrs, Jardines, and others, ruled on the Borders, and set both their own government and that of England at defiance. Sir Ralph Sadler, who was posted at Berwick by Queen Elizabeth to watch the movements of the Scotch court, and to corrupt all the nobles, went amongst these bold Border chiefs, and gives some lively descriptions in his despatches of their mode of life; their drinking, gaming, riding, and open contempt of all authority. During the minority of James VI., the daring of the Border chiefs rose to an enormous pitch. Buccleuch, with his followers, on one occasion, assisted by Lord Claud Hamilton, seized the Regent Lennox, and were very near getting possession of the young king in Stirling. Failing in this, they killed the Regent. Morton, who succeeded Lennox as Regent, managed to sow dissension amongst the Border chiefs, and made an attempt to surprise Jedburgh and Ferniehurst, but was repulsed. After the death of Morton the full licence of the Border revived. A son of the Earl of Bedford was, in 1585, killed in one of their frays by Kerr of Fernichurst, which, at the demand of Elizabeth, brought that doughty chief to a dungeon, where he died. After that, Francis Stuart, an illegitimate son of James V., who had been created Earl of Bothwell, on the forfeiture of the infamous Bothwell, husband of Queen Mary, made great disturbance on the Border; he was highly popular with the men of Jedburgh and Teviotdale, and even attempted to feize the perfon of James VI. in his palace of Holyrood. In the meantime, the chiefs in the neighbourhood of Jedburgh and the Middle Marches were fighting with each other for the provoftry of Jedburgh, in which affray Kerr of Ancram, a follower of Ferniehurft, was killed. Such was the favage condition of this neighbourhood down to the very epoch of James VI.'s afcent of the Englifh throne. Robert Carr, the infamous favourite of James I., was third fon of Sir Thomas Kerr, of Ferniehurft Caftle, which is only a mile and a half from Jedburgh.

The caftle of Jedburgh was fo formidable a protection to the infubordinate Borderers in thefe difturbed times, that in the beginning of the fixteenth century the Government refolved to deftroy it; and the work appeared fo enormous, from its ponderous ftrength, that it was propofed to lay a tax of two pennies on every hearth in Scotland to defray the expenfe. On the fite was raifed the county gaol, which is ftill called the caftle. A fingular occurrence took place in a cell of this caftle, in the reign of Charles I., which led to a yet more remarkable one, indicative of the ftill lawlefs condition of the times. We give it in the words of Sir Walter Scott:—

"In the reign of Charles I., when the mofs-trooping practices were not entirely difcontinued, the tower of Gilnockie, in the parifh of Cannoby, was occupied by William Armftrong, called, for diftinction's fake, Chriftie's Will, a lineal defcendant of the famous John Armftrong, of Gilnockie, executed by James VI. The hereditary love of plunder had defcended to this perfon with the family manfion; and, upon fome marauding party, he was feized and imprifoned in the tolbooth of Jedburgh. The Earl of Traquair, Lord High Treafurer, happening to vifit Jedburgh, and knowing Chriftie's

Will, inquired the cause of his confinement. Will replied that he was imprisoned for stealing two *tethers* (halters); but, upon being more closely interrogated, acknowledged that there were two *delicate colts* at the end of them. The joke, such as it was, amused the earl, who exerted his interest, and succeeded in releasing Will from bondage. Some time afterwards, a lawsuit of importance to Lord Traquair was to be decided in the Court of Session, and there was every reason to believe that judgment would turn upon the voice of the presiding judge, who has a casting vote, in case of an equal division among his brethren. The opinion of the President was unfavourable to Lord Traquair, and the point was, therefore, to keep him out of the way when the question should be tried. In this dilemma, the earl had recourse to Christie's Will, who at once offered his services to kidnap the President. Upon due scrutiny he found it was the judge's practice to take the air on horseback on the Sands of Leith, without an attendant. In one of these excursions, Christie's Will, who had long watched his opportunity, ventured to accost the President and engage him in conversation. His address and language were so amusing, that he decoyed the President into an unfrequented and furzy common, called the Frigate Whins, where, riding suddenly up to him, he pulled him from his horse, muffled him in a large cloak, which he had provided, and rode off with the luckless judge trussed up behind him. Will crossed the country with great expedition, by paths known only to persons of his description, and deposited his weary and terrified burden in an old castle in Annandale, called the Tower of Graham. The judge's horse being found, it was concluded that he had thrown his rider into the sea, his friends went into mourning, and a successor was appointed to his office. Meanwhile, the poor President spent a heavy time in the vault of the castle. He was imprisoned and solitary, receiving his food through an aperture in the wall, and never hearing the sound of a human voice, save when a shepherd called his dog by the name of *Batty*, and when a female domestic called upon *Maudge*, the cat. These, he concluded, were invocations of spirits; for he held himself to be in the dungeon of a sorcerer. At length, after three months had elapsed, the lawsuit was decided in favour of Lord Traquair, and Will was directed to set the President at liberty. Accordingly, he entered the vault at the dead of the night, seized the President, muffled him once more in the cloak, without speaking a single word, and, using the same mode of transportation, conveyed him to Leith Sands, and set down the astonished judge at the very spot where he had taken him up. The joy of his friends, and the less agreeable surprise of his successor, may easily be conceived, when he appeared in court to reclaim his office and honours. All embraced his own persuasion, that he had been spirited away by witchcraft; nor could he himself be convinced of the contrary, until, many years afterwards, happening to travel in Annandale, his ears were saluted once more with the sounds of *Maudge* and *Batty*, the only notes which had solaced his long confinement. This led to a discovery of the whole story; but, in those disorderly times, it was only laughed at as a fair *ruse de guerre.*

" Wild and strange as this tradition may seem, there is little doubt of its foundation in fact. The judge upon whose person this extraordinary stratagem was practised, was Sir Alexander Gibson, Lord Durie, collector of the reports well known in the Scottish law under the title of *Durie's Decisions*. He was advanced to the station of an ordinary Lord of Session, 10th of July, 1621, and died at his own house of Durie, July, 1646. Betwixt these periods, this whimsical adventure muſt have happened; a date which correſponds with that of the tradition."

Another and the popular verſion of this extraordinary abduction is given in the ballad of Chriſtie's Will. There the Borderer, being engaged by Lord Traquair,—

> He lighted at Lord Durie's door,
>   And there he knocked moſt manfullie;
> And up and ſpake Lord Durie ſae ſtout,
>   "What tidings, thou ſtalwart groom, to me?"
>
> "The faireſt lady in Teviotdale
>   Has ſent, moſt reverent ſir, for thee;
> She pleas at the Seſſion for her land a' haill,
>   And fain ſhe would plead her cauſe to thee."
>
> "But how can I to that lady ride,
>   With ſaving of my dignitie?"
> "O, a curch and mantle ye may wear,
>   And in my cloak ſall muffled be."
>
> Wi' curch on head and cloak owre face,
>   He mounted the judge on a palfrey fine:
> He rode away, a right round pace,
>   And Chriſtie's Will held the bridle reyn.
>
> The Lothian Edge they were not o'er,
>   When they heard bugles bauldly ring,
> And, hunting over Middleton Moor,
>   They met, I ween, our noble king.
>
> When Willie looked upon the king,
>   I wot a frightened man was he!
> But even auld Durie was ſtartled mair,
>   For tyning of his dignitie.
>
> The king he croſſed himſelf, I wis,
>   When as the pair came riding bye—
> "An uglier crone, and a ſturdier loon
>   I think were never ſeen with eye!"
>
> Willie has hied to the tower of Græme,
>   He took auld Durie on his back,
> He ſhot him down to the dungeon deep,
>   Which garred his auld banes gie mony a crack.

> For nineteen days and nineteen nights,
> Of fun, or moon, or midnight ftern,
> Auld Durie never faw a blink,
> The lodging was fo dark and dern.
>
> He thought the warlocks o' the rofy-crofs
> Had fanged him in their nets fae faft ;
> Or that the gipfies' glamoured gang
> Had laired his learning at the laft.

Having now recounted the incidents of ftormy times which led to the deftruction of the caftle of Jedburgh, and to the ruin of the abbey, which was burnt by the Earl of Hereford in 1545, we will take a curfory glance at the remains of this once magnificent monaftery, as they yet exift. The chapter-houfe, cloifters, and other parts have perifhed, and the church alone furvives, and, in the form of a crofs, extends from eaft to weft 230 feet. The choir is much dilapidated, no doubt from being of a much greater age than the reft. The two lower ftories confift of maffive pillars and femicircular arches, with the diagonal or zigzag mouldings of Saxon architecture ; whilft the upper windows are of early Englifh, having been evidently added at a more recent period. The north tranfept is entire, pre-fenting traceried pointed windows, which are efpecially of great fize and beauty. Above the interfection of the tranfepts with the nave and choir, a large fquare tower rifes on four pillars to the height of 100 feet, furmounted by projecting battlements, and crowned with turrets and pinnacles. The nave, meafuring a hundred feet in length, prefents on each fide three tiers of arches ; the firft, opening into the aifle, confifts of pointed arches, deeply receffed and richly moulded, fupported by cluftered columns, with fculptured capitals ; the fecond, which opened into the galleries, confifts of beautifully moulded femi-circular aifles, with two pointed arches inferted in each ; and the third, of elegantly pointed windows. The lofty weftern front poſſeſſes a Norman door of uncommon beauty, the archway exhibiting a profuſion of ornamented mouldings ſupported by ſlender receding pillars to the depth of ſeven feet and a half. Above it is a large window with a ſemicircular arch, flanked by ſmall blank pointed arches, on long, ſlender ſhafts, and this ſurmounted by a beautiful St. Catherine's Wheel. On the ſouth fide of the choir there is a chapel, which was formerly uſed as a grammar-ſchool, and there the poet Thomſon was educated. But the chief beauty of the building is the Norman door which formed the ſouthern entrance to the church from the cloiſters. This is unrivalled in Scotland for the ſymmetry of its proportions and the elegance of its workmanſhip. Its ſculptured mouldings, ſpringing from ſlender ſhafts, with capitals richly wreathed, preſent the figures of men, animals, and flowers of the moſt admirable delicacy and minuteneſs. Altogether, the late Archibald Elliot, architect, pronounced this, in a ſtatiſtical account of Scotland, the moſt perfect and beautiful ſpecimen of the Saxon and Early Gothic in Scotland.

The neighbourhood of Jedburgh is well worthy of poſſeſsing beautiful remains of the old times and their arts. The town lies on ground riſing from the weſt bank of the Jed, and is ſurrounded by pleaſant gardens and cheerful villas ſcattered amongſt them and their orchards. Around riſe wooded ſlopes, and at a diſtance is deſcried the dark bulk of Carter Fell. Above the caſtle hill riſes alſo the Dunion; northward is ſeen Hartrigg, the ſeat of Lord Campbell; and farther off the heights of Penilheugh, with its Wellington monument. The neighbouring dale of Teviot is extremely fine, and varied by its hills and ſlopes, and maſſes of wood, remains of the ancient foreſt. The Jed, as well as the Teviot, charmed Burns, who viſited Jedburgh in 1789, and ſung of " Eden ſcenes on cryſtal Jed." Fernichurſt Caſtle, now in ruins, occupying a steep bank overhanging the Jed, and enriched with ancient woods, is a fine object. On the Jed, at Southdean, under Carter Fell, lived the poet Thomson's father, when the embryo bard was only two years old, and there he spent his

JEDBURGH: WESTERN GATEWAY.

boyhood. From this place his father sent him, mounted behind a servant man, to Edinburgh, to the university; but the town was by no means to the taste of the author of "The Seasons:" he had found his way back to the manse on foot before the man had got there on horseback, and declared to the aftonifhed family, that he was fure he could ftudy as well in Southdean as in Edinburgh. Dr. Somerville, the hiftorian of William and Anne, was for more than fifty years minifter of Jedburgh; and there was born the celebrated Mrs. Somer-

JEDBURGH: SOUTH PORCH.

ville. It is the native place, alfo, of Sir David Brewfter; and with thefe names we bid adieu to

> The hoary peaks of Scotland, that give birth
> To Teviot's ftream, to Annan, Tweed, and Clyde.

Dryburgh Abbey.

Let us explore the ruined abbey's choir;
Its fretted roof and windows of rich tracery,
The sculptured tombs o'ergrown with shrubs and brambles,
Midst broken arches, graves, and gloomy vaults:
Or view the castle of some ancient thane,
Its hall, its dungeons, and embattled towers,
Mantled with ivy.

E are now come into the immediate vicinity of the great romancer of Abbotsford, and to the place which, for its beauty, as well as some ancestral associations, he chose for his burial-place. To both these influences—those of nature and of ancestry—no man was ever more subject. He raised his great fame on their united strength, he broke down the fair fortune which his genius, employed on such themes, had won, and darkened his latter days, and taxed his failing strength, in the endeavour to confer on his name and children higher honours, rather secular than literary. With these few failings, what a genial glory envelopes his memory, and what a like glory of all rainbow hues has he cast over the whole country which surrounded his favourite abode! He has collected all that history, tradition, ballad, and legend have bequeathed to this part of Scotland, and has added new charms to them. The personal memory of the great romancer, with all his poetic and historic tastes, is now for ever interwoven with the scenes and stories, chivalrous or monastic, that he loved.

Dryburgh lies amid the scenes in which he not only took such peculiar delight, but which furnished him themes both for his poems and romances, and which were rich in those old songs and narratives of Border feats and raids which he has preserved in his Border Minstrelsy. Melrose, the Eildon Hills, the haunt of Thomas of Ercildoune, Jedburgh, Yetholm, the Cowdenknowes, the Yarrow, and Ettrick, all lie on different sides within a circle of twenty miles, and most of them much nearer. Smailholme Tower, the scene of some of Scott's youthful days, and of his ballad of "The Eve of St. John," is also one of these. Grose tells us that "The ruins of Dryburgh Monastery are beautifully situated on a peninsula formed by the Tweed, ten miles above Kelso, and three below Melrose, on the south-western confine of the county of Berwick.

"St. Modan, who was one of the first Christian missionaries in Britain, was abbot of Dryburgh about the year 522, and made apostolical excursions into the north-western parts of Scotland, particularly in the districts of Stirling and Dumbarton, where his memory is still to be traced in popular tradition. There is some reason to conjecture that on this spot there had been more anciently a Druidical establishment, because the Celtic or Gaelic etymology of the name, Darach-bruach, or Darachbrugh, or Dryburgh, can be no otherwise interpreted than as the bank of the sacred grove of oaks, or the settlemen of the Druids; and we know that it was usual for the first planters of Christianity in Pagan countries to choose such sacred haunts for the propagation of the gospel.

"Bede, however, in his ecclesiastical history, is silent on this subject; and, as more than a century had elapsed from the days of Modan to those of the venerable historian, it is probable that the religious refidence had been transferred to Melrofe long before he compofed his annals."

The new Abbey of Dryburgh had the credit of being founded in 1150, by David I., who was fond of the reputation of a founder of abbeys; Holyrood Abbey, Melrofe Abbey, Kelfo Abbey, Jedburgh Abbey, and others, having David I. ftated as their founder. However it might be in other cafes, and in fome of them he was merely the reftorer, the real founders of Dryburgh were Hugh de Morville, Lord of Lauderdale, and Conftable of Scotland, and his wife, Beatrice de Beauchamp. They obtained a charter of confirmation from King David, in which he affumes the character of founder. The chronicle of Melrofe, however, clearly fhows who were the founders, and places David in his true pofition of patron only. The cemetery of the abbey was confecrated on St. Martin's Day, in the year of its completion, as the chronicle obferves, "ne dæmones in iis graffarentur." Hugh de Morville brought monks of the Premonftratenfian order from Alnwick, to occupy it, in 1152. A monk of this houfe, Rodulphus de Strode, travelled through England, France, Germany, Italy, and Paleftine. Dempfter calls him a poet of eminence, and efteemed by Chaucer; that he was of the ftaunch old Catholic fchool is fhown by his being a determined antagonift of Wycliffe and his doctrines.

Edward II., in his invafion of Scotland in 1323, burnt down Dryburgh Abbey, as he had done that of Melrofe in the preceding year; and both thefe magnificent houfes were reftored principally at the coft of Robert Bruce. It was again deftroyed by the Englifh in 1544, by Sir George Bowes and Sir Brian Latoun, as Melrofe was alfo. Amongft the moft diftinguifhed of its abbots we may mention Andrew Fordun, Bifhop of Moray, and afterwards Archbifhop of St.

Andrews, and ambaffador to France, and who held fome of the moft important offices under James IV. and James V. The favours conferred upon him were in proportion to his confequence in the ftate. Along with this Abbey of Dryburgh, he held in commendam thofe of Pittenweem, Coldingham, and Dunfermline. He refigned Dryburgh to James Ogilvie, of the family of Defkford. Ogilvie was alfo confiderably employed in offices of diplomacy, both at London and Paris.

Sir Walter Scott, in his Introduction to the Border Minftrelfy, gives fome curious particulars regarding this abbot from a MS. hiftory of the Halliburtons of Mertoun or Newmains. Thefe Halliburtons held fome lands under the abbey, about which contentions repeatedly took place betwixt the abbot and his tenants. In the rude fpirit of the times, they proceeded to fettle their differences by arms inftead of by lawyers' tongues. Blood having been fhed between them, the king called the matter before him, and made an award dated at Stirling, in May, 1535, which was, that, as the Halliburtons were good fubjects of the king, ftout men-at-arms, and brave Borderers againft England, they fhould be left in quiet poffeffion of their lands, and fhould be good fervants to the venerable father the abbot, as their predeceffors had been to the venerable father's predeceffors. So eafy an award did not promife much peace, nor did it infure it. A marriage, indeed, was arranged betwixt the daughter—a natural daughter, we may fuppofe—of the abbot, Elizabeth Stewart, and Walter Halliburton, one of the family of Newmains; but this did not extinguifh the feud. The offspring of this marriage was one daughter, named Elizabeth Halliburton. To keep the property in the family, the Halliburtons determined to marry her to one of her coufins; but the arbitrary old abbot did not confent to this fcheme, but had his grandchild carried off by force, and married her to

Alexander Erſkine, a relative of his own, and brother to the laird of Balgony. This daring act of the abbot kindled afreſh the ancient feud betwixt the abbey and the Halliburtons, which continued to rage till the diſſolution of the houſe.

The Erſkines ſeemed to keep firm hold of the Abbey of Dryburgh, and Adam Erſkine, one of Abbot James's ſucceſſors, was, under George Buchanan, a ſub-preceptor to James VI. This James I. of England diſſolved the abbey in 1604, and conferred it and its lands, together with the abbeys and eſtates of Cambuſkenneth and Inchmahornæ, on John Erſkine, Earl of Mar, who was made, on this occaſion, alſo Baron of Cardroſs, which barony was compoſed of the property of theſe three monaſteries. In this line, Dryburgh deſcended to the lords of Buchan. The Earls of Buchan, at one time, ſold it to the Halliburtons of Mortoun, from whom it was purchaſed by Colonel Tod, whoſe heirs again ſold it to the Earl of Buchan in 1786. This eccentric nobleman bequeathed it to his ſon, Sir David Erſkine, at whoſe death in 1837 it reverted to the Buchan family.

Two monaſteries in Ireland, the Abbey of Druin-la-Croix in the County of Armagh, and the Abbey of Woodburn in the County of Antrim, acknowledged Dryburgh as their mother. A copy of the Liber S. Mariæ de Dryburgh is in the Advocates' Library in Edinburgh, containing all its ancient charters. Such are the main points of hiſtory connected with Dryburgh; but, when we open the ballad lore of the South of Scotland, we find this fine old place figuring repeatedly and prominently.

Maitland, of the ballad of "Auld Maitland," was a benefactor to Dryburgh. This Sir Richard Mautlant or Maitland, of Lauder or Thirleſtane, gave lands to the abbey at Haubent-ſide in his demeſne of Thirleſtane. He alſo gave to the ſame convent other lands held by Walter de Gilling in Thirleſtane, and pasture for forty sheep, sixty cows, and twenty horses. This stout old Maitland is represented as holding his castle of Thirlestane against the English army, headed by an imaginary nephew of Edward I.

> As they fared up o'er Lammermore,
>   They burned baith up and doun,
> Until they came to a darksome house,
>   Some call it Leader Toun.
>
> "Wha hauds this house?" young Edward cried,
>   "Or wha geist ower to me?"
> A grey-haired knight set up his head,
>   And crackit richt crousely:—
>
> "Of Scotland's king I haud my house;
>   He pays me meat and fee;
> And I will keep my guid auld house,
>   While my house will keep me."

The Eildon Hill, on which Thomas of Ercildoune had his interview with the fairy queen, looks down upon you on your right hand as you go from Melrose to Dryburgh. Cowdenknowes, which gave rise to the fine old ballad of the "Broom o' the Cowdenknowes," Bemerside, and Merton House, the seat of Scott of Harden, one of Sir Walter's relatives, are not far off. Many of these associations Scott has woven into his ballad of the "Eve of St. John." The Lady of Smailholme Tower is made to say to her paramour:—

> O fear not the priest, who sleepeth to the east!
>   For to Dryburgh the way he hath ta'en;
> And there to say mass, till three days do pass,
>   For the soul of a knight that is slain.

And the Lord, the Baron of Smailholme, says to his page:—

> Where fair Tweed flows round holy Melrose,
>   And Eildon slopes to the plain,
> Full three nights ago, by some secret foe,
>   That gay gallant was slain.

> The varying light deceived thy fight,
>   And the wild winds drowned the name ;
> For the Dryburgh bells ring, and the white monks do fing,
>   For Richard of Coldinghame.

Into the guilty details of the liafon of the Lady of Smailholme and this Sir Richard of Coldinghame, Scott has introduced warning phenomena, drawn probably from fome of his German reading, but more particularly from the ftory of Lady Beresford and Lord Tyrone. In the apparition fcene,—

> Love maftered fear—her brow fhe croffed;
> "How, Richard, haft thou fped ?
> And art thou faved, or art thou loft ?"
>   The vifion fhook his head.
>
> " Who fpilleth life fhall forfeit life,
>   So bid thy lord believe ;
> That lawlefs love is guilt above,
>   This awful fign receive."
>
> He laid his left palm on an oaken beam,
>   His right upon her hand ;
> The lady fhrunk and fainting funk,
>   For it fcorched like a fiery brand.
>
> The fable fcore of fingers four
>   Remains on that board impreffed ;
> And for ever more that lady wore
>   A covering on her wrift.
>
> There is a nun in Dryburgh bower
>   Ne'er looks upon the fun ;
> There is a monk in Melrofe tower,
>   He fpeaketh word to none.
>
> That nun who ne'er beholds the day,
>   That monk who fpeaks to none—
> That nun was Smaylho'mes lady gay,
>   That monk the bold baron

To this ghoftly ballad Sir Walter appends this ghoftly anecdote :—" About fifty years ago, an unfortunate female wanderer took up her residence in a dark vault, among the ruins of Dryburgh Abbey, which, during the day, she never quitted. When night fell, she issued from this miserable habitation, and went to the house of Mr. Halliburton, of Newmains, the editor's great-grandfather, or to that of Mr. Erskine, of Shielfield, two gentlemen of the neighbourhood. From their charity she obtained such necessaries as she could only be prevailed upon to accept. At twelve each night she lighted her candle, and returned to her vault, assuring her friendly neighbours that, during her absence, her habitation was arranged by a spirit, to whom she gave the uncouth name of Fat Lips; describing him as a little man, wearing heavy iron shoes, with which he trampled the clay floor of the vault to dispel the damps. This circumstance caused her to be regarded, by the well-informed, with compassion, as deranged in her understanding; and by the vulgar, with some degree of terror. The cause of her adopting this extraordinary mode of life she would never explain. It was, however, believed to have been occasioned by a vow that, during the absence of a man to whom she was attached, she would never look upon the sun. Her lover never returned, he fell during the civil war of 1745-6, and she never more would behold the light of day.

"The vault, or rather dungeon, in which this unfortunate woman lived and died, passes still by the name of the supernatural being with which its gloom was tenanted by her disturbed imagination, and few of the neighbouring peasants dare enter it at night."

Having now noticed the history and tradition of Dryburgh, let us take a view of it as it now exists. Grose says,—"The freestone of which the monastery of Dryburgh and the most elegant parts of the abbey of Melrose were built, is of a most beautiful colour and texture, and has defied the influence of the weather for more than fix centuries; nor is the fharpnefs of the fculpture in the leaft affected by the ravages of time. The quarry from which it was taken is ftill fuccefsfully worked at Dryburgh, and no ftone in the ifland feems more perfectly adapted for the purpofes of architecture, as it hardens by age, and is not fubject to be corroded or decompofed by the weather, fo that it might even be ufed for the cutting of bas-reliefs and of ftatues." He adds:—

" The ftate of this ruin, when viewed by Mr. Pennant, in

DRYBURGH ABBEY.

the year 1769, was a very little remains of the church, but much of the convent; the refectory, supported by two pillars, several vaults, and other offices; part of the cloister walls; and a fine radiated window of stone work. Since this account was written, the refectory, supported by the two pillars above-mentioned, has fallen; but the gable-ends are still remaining; in one of which is the fine circular radiated window, described by Mr. Pennant, at present finely mantled with ivy."

As the remains of the abbey have since been carefully preserved, they present still much the same aspect as at Grose's visit in 1797. When I visited this lovely ruin and lovely neighbourhood in 1845, I walked from Melrose, a distance of between three and four miles. Leaving the Eildon Hills on my right, and following the course of the Tweed, I saw, as I progressed, Cowdenknowes, Bemerside, and other spots famous in Border song. Issuing from a steep and woody lane, I came out on a broad bend of the river, with a wide strand of gravel and stones on this side, showing with what force the wintry torrents rushed along here. Opposite rose lofty and finely-wooded banks. Amid the trees on that side shone out a little temple of the Muses, where they are represented as consecrating Thomson the poet. Farther off, on a hill, stands a gigantic statue of William Wallace, which was originally intended for Burns; but, the stone being too large, it was thought by the eccentric Lord Buchan, who erected it, a pity to cut it down. Another still more striking monument of the activity of Lord Buchan are the remains of a chain-bridge which he had erected across the river. This would have been a great convenience to the neighbourhood had it been durable; but a tempest tore it to pieces, and there stood up the great white wood frames to which the bridge was attached, the two main chains still stretching across, but the fragments of others dangling in the air, looking moſt ghaſtly and ruinous. So it was in 1845, and ſo it ſtill ſeems to continue; for Walter White, who viſited the ſpot in 1858, or 1859, found theſe ruins of the bridge ſtill unremoved.

I was ferried over by two women, who were by no means ſorry that the winds and floods had carried my Lord Buchan's bridge away, as it reſtored their buſineſs of putting people over. I then aſcended a lane from the ferry, and found myſelf in front of an apparently old caſtle gateway; but, from the Latin inſcription over it, diſcovered that it was alſo erected by the ſame ſingular Lord Buchan, as the entrance to a Pomarium, or, in plain Engliſh, an orchard, dedicated to his honoured parents, who, I ſuppoſe, like our firſt parents, were particularly fond of apples. That his parents or himſelf might enjoy all the apples, he had, under the Latin dedication, placed a ſimple Engliſh menace of ſteel traps and ſpring guns. I ſtill advanced through a pleaſant ſcene of trees and cottages, of rich graſſy crofts, with cattle lying luxuriouſly in them, and amid a huſh of repoſe, indicative of a monaſtic ſcene. Having found a guide to the ruins, at a cottage near the river, I was led acroſs a young orchard towards them, the two old gables and the fine circular window ſhowing themſelves above the foliage. I found the interior of the ruins carpeted by ſoft turf, and two rows of cedars growing in the church, marking where the aiſles formerly ran. The cloiſters and ſouth tranſept were ſtill entire, and diſplayed much fine workmanſhip. The great circular window is eſpecially lovely, formed of five ſtars cut in ſtone, ſo that the open centre within them forms a roſe. The light ſeen through this charming window produced a fine effect. The chapter-houſe was alſo entire, the floor being now only of earth; and a circle was drawn in the centre, where the remains of the founder and his lady lie. Here again, however, the fantaſtic old Lord Buchan had interfered, and a ſtatue of Locke, reading in an open book, and pointing to his own forehead, one of Inigo Jones, and one of Newton, made you wonder what they were doing there. So totally without regard to fitneſs did this half-crazy nobleman put down his ſuppoſed ornaments. The wonder is that his ſucceſſor had not removed theſe, and ſome ſtatues or buſts which had as little buſineſs on the ſpot.

But the charm of the place in every ſenſe was the grave of Scott. It was in the Lady aiſle, and occupies two arches of it; and the adjoining ſpace under the next arch is the burial-place of the Erſkines, as Scott's burial-place was that of his anceſtors the Halliburtons. The whole, with the tier of ſmall ſectional Norman arches above, form a glorious tomb much reſembling one of the chapel tombs in Wincheſter Cathedral. Taken in connection with the fine ruins, and the finer natural ſcenery around, no ſpot can be ſuppoſed more ſuitable for the reſting-place of the remains of the great minſtrel and romancer, who ſo delighted in the natural, hiſtoric, and legendary charms of the neighbourhood, and who added ſtill greater ones to them himſelf.

And yet there is a ſerious drawback to this feeling. The place is private property; and, though the public is admitted to it, it was then, and would appear from recent accounts to be yet, done in a ſpirit that is anything but liberal and courteous. I found the perſons who ſhowed the place particularly uncourteous, and, on ſtating this in the neighbourhood, was aſſured that this was a general experience. In fact, nothing could be more marked than the pleaſantneſs with which Melroſe and Abbotsford were ſhown to me, and the ſullen diſcourteſy and impatience of the guides here; and this could not be the caſe were the ſpirit of their employers of a more liberal stamp. Walter White, in his recent visit, says, that he persuaded his companion, an American, to linger awhile in the ruin; but the maiden, the guide, " came back and spoke of regulations which forbid uncontrolled liberty, so, to save her the trouble of watching, we departed. On our way back to the ferry, the American finds further fault with the criticisms of one of his countrymen on the Abbey, and does not see why the unhappy one in the boat complained of Jack-in-office." This Jack-in-office had, it is clear, retained the same character as my Jack-in-office, thirteen years before.

Since my visit, a massive tomb, of Aberdeen granite, has been placed over the remains of Sir Walter and Lady Scott, and those of their eldest son. A railway also now makes the place much more accessible, the station for Dryburgh being at the village of Newtown, on the other side of the river. Near St. Boswell's, opposite to Dryburgh, has also been lately erected a bridge over the Tweed, opening up the communication betwixt the north and south side of the river, and thus enabling the tourist to explore at greater convenience the scenes of ancient loves and feuds, and the haunts of Scott. Here his dust lies amid the objects redolent of his fame, and within a few miles, near Makerstoun, a view may be obtained, from a hill, of Smailholme Tower, where the poet passed some of the years of his boyhood, and the memory of which he has perpetuated in one of the epistles which introduce each Canto of Marmion:—

>It was a barren scene and wild,
>Where naked cliffs were rudely piled;
>But, ever and anon, between,
>Lay velvet tufts of loveliest green;
>And well the lonely infant knew
>Recesses where the wall-flower grew,
>And honeysuckle loved to crawl
>Up the low crag and ruined wall,

I deemed such nooks the sweetest shade
The sun in all his round surveyed;
And still I thought that shattered tower
The mightiest work of human power;
And marvelled, as the aged hind
With some strange tale bewitch'd my mind,
Of forayers, who, with headlong force,
Down from that strength had spurred their horse,
Their southern rapine to renew
Far in the distant Cheviots blue,
And home returning, filled the hall,
With revel, wassail, rout, and brawl.

The Rock of Cashel.

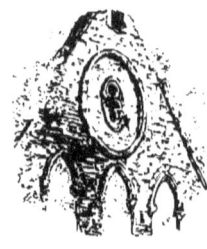

ONE of the moſt intereſting places in Ireland is the Rock of Caſhel, in Tipperary. It ſtands boldly in the midſt of a vaſt champagne, crowned by a cluſter of ruins which unite ſome of the moſt attractive reminiscences, and ſome of the moſt exquiſite eccleſiaſtical architecture in the iſland. The character of ſcene in which the Rock and Tower of Caſhel ſtand is, as ſtated by Frazer, beſt ſeen from the neighbouring hill of Killough. "The hill of Killough is eaſy of aſcent, and, from its ſuperior altitude, a much better view is obtained than from the Rock of Caſhel; beſides, this hill, and the rocky range running from it, form a viſual barrier to the view northward from the rock. If the day is favourable for diſtant proſpects, the view is bounded only by the ſurrounding high lands which blend with the diſtant horizon. Eaſtward, the detached and very remarkable mountain of Slievenaman ſtretches acroſs, and prevents the eye ranging down the valley of the Suir; and the low and ſoftly rounded hills of Kilkenny, ſweeping from Killenaule to Freſhford, and thence to Durrow, ſeem to diſplay and prolong the diſtant perſpective. Northward, the range of hills generally known as the Slievebloom mountains, running from Tullamore to Roſcrea, and, nearer, the Devil's Bit range of hills, blending with the Keeper mountains, take up the

ROCK OF CASHEL: GENERAL VIEW.

boundary line from Roscrea to Limerick, lapping over the Clare highlands beyond the Upper Shannon. Weftward, the hills iffue from the Lower Shannon, at Shanagolden, and run nearly at right angles to its courfe acrofs the country to Charleville; from whence fpring in a foutherly direction the Caftle Oliver mountains, connecting with the near and more lofty Galtees, by far the fineft of our inland mountain ranges. Due fouth, and more within the reach of the unaided eye, may be feen a portion of the Munavuleagh and Knockmealedown mountains, which run in a wefterly direction from Carrick-on-Suir to Kilworth."

In the centre of this grand panorama ſtands the rock, with the town cloſely crouched at its feet. On the ſummit of the rock riſes a ſplendid group of ruins, confiſting of the cathedral, Cormack's chapel, and the caſtle and monaſtery. Around theſe ruins an area of about three acres of the richeſt ſward has been encloſed, which is open to the public; and the pariſh ſexton, who acts as the cicerone, is at hand to ſhow the interior. The cathedral forms the centre of the group of theſe celebrated ruins, which are unparalleled in Ireland for picturefque beauty and antiquarian intereſt. It is a noble remnant of early pointed Gothic, and contains many intereſting relics. The caſtellated building adjoining forms externally a part of, and is internally connected with, the cathedral, and appears to have been a place of great ſtrength in thoſe days when princely eccleſiaſtics aſſumed the powers of lords temporal as well as ſpiritual. To the north ſtands one of the old Round Towers, and, on the ſouth ſide, Cormack's Chapel.

This famous chapel was built by Cormack M'Carthy, King of Munſter, in 1136. In its external figure it ſtrikingly reſembles thoſe far more ancient churches of the Iriſh Chriſtian fathers who, from the fifth century, continued to evangelize and civilize the rude people, till the Roman hierarchy came in, roſe over their heads, and put them down. We have already had to notice the labours and domiciles of this ſimple and devoted race of Chriſtian fathers at Iona and Lindisfarne, who ſpread themſelves thence all over Europe. As in the places mentioned, ſo in Ireland, they generally ſought the wildeſt and moſt deſolate ſpots for their reſidences, as more fitted for religious contemplation, from having nothing to call off the attention by its amenity. They had ſuch at Smerwick Harbour, in the county of Kerry, at Biſhop's Iſland, near Kilkee, upon the coaſt of Clare, ſtyled in Iriſh, " Oiléan-an-

Eafpoig-gor-taigh," *i.e.*, the ifle of the hungry or ftarving bifhop. This was a barren, precipitous rock, environed with perpendicular or overhanging cliffs, about 250 feet in height, and containing about three-quarters of an acre of furface, to which accefs is moft difficult, and only to be effected by a fkilful climber, and after a continuance of calm weather. There was another fuch fecluded feat of piety on the ifland of Ard-Oiléan, or Eye Ifland, off the coaft of Connemara. The only companions of the holy fathers on this ifland were the fea-birds, which built there in thoufands, and a few martins. So lonely and defolate was the place, that even thefe creatures feemed to have loft their dread of man. Again, Saint Senan had, in the fixth century, a very primitive church on Inis Cathaigh or Scattery Ifland, the Iona of the South of Ireland.

In moft of thefe, the earlieft erections were fimply fquare huts, the gables tapering up from the ground to the eaves, and then covered in by flabs of ftone gradually approximating, till they met at the ridge. The windows were very fmall, very few, and alfo contracting upwards. The doors did the fame, being fometimes not fix feet high, yet two feet four inches wide at the bottom, and only one foot nine inches at the top, which was finifhed, not by an arch, but by a flat lintel. Others were circular, with the bafe low, and the roof a high cone of ftones laid to contract at every frefh layer till they terminated in a point at the top. Thefe little dwellings and churches were fuch as the moft unfkilled perfon could erect, and yet were fo ftrong as to refift the force of the tempeft of the wild locations in which they were raifed.

As time and architecture advanced, the churches, though ftill fmall, became fquare, with high-pitched ftone roofs, and doors and windows ftill fhowing the fame ftyle of contracting upwards, but now often finifhed by arches, round or pointed.

The walls were very thick, and therefore the windows were widened, or difplayed inwards to admit more light. Such are the remains of the ancient Irifh churches in the romantic valley of Glendalough in Wicklow, of the ftructure called St. Kevin's Kitchen in the fame valley, of Killiney Church, about nine miles from Dublin; of the Church of Kilternan, about fix miles from Dublin on the Ennifkerry Road, of St. Columb's Houfe at Kells, County Meath, and of St. Flannan's Houfe at Killaloe.

The roofs of thefe churches did not depend on the mutual fupport of the ftone flabs forming them, but were borne on ftone arches. It is curious that, as the Norman period approached, the windows and doors of thefe churches were found to be ornamented with the zig-zag or chevron moulding, had receffed arches, and pillars furmounted with capitals prefenting fculptured faces, mingled with the remains of their own old ftyle, their upward narrowing doors and peculiar pillars. Norman, whatever it did in England before the Conqueft, has been fhown by Wakeman to have been modifying the Irifh ecclefiaftical architecture for fome time. After that period, the Norman ftyle prevailed more purely, and no finer proof of this exifts than in St. Cormack's Chapel at Cafhel. With the exception of the Round Tower, it is the moft ancient ftructure on the rock. The numerous ornaments, grotefque heads, and other curious fculptures which adorn the arches, columns, and pilafters, are all uniform in ftyle, and that ftyle is diftinctly Norman. The plan is a nave and chancel, with a fquare tower on each fide, at their junction. The fouthern tower is ornamented externally with fix projecting bands, three of which are continued along the fide walls of the ftructure; and it is finifhed at the top by a plain parapet, the mafonry of which is different from that of the other portions, and evidently of a later period. The northern tower remains in its original ſtate, and is covered with a pyramidal cap of ſtone. An almoſt endleſs variety of Norman decorations appear upon the arches and other features of the building, both within and without. Both nave and chancel are roofed with a ſemi-circular arch, reſting upon ſquare ribs, which ſpring from a ſeries of maſſive ſemi-columns, ſet at equal diſtances againſt the walls. The baſes of theſe ſemi-columns are on a level with the capitals of the choir arch, the abacus of which is continued as a ſtring courſe round the interior of the building. The walls of both nave and chancel beneath the ſtring courſe are ornamented with a row of ſemi-circular arches, ſlightly receſſed, and enriched with chevron, fillet, and other ornaments and mouldings. Thoſe of the nave ſpring from ſquare impoſts reſting upon piers, while thoſe in the chancel have pillars and well-formed capitals. There are ſmall crofts, to which acceſs is gained by a ſpiral ſtair in the northern tower, between the arches over both nave and chancel, and the external roof. Theſe little apartments were probably uſed as dormitories by the eccleſiaſtics. A ſimilar croft in the church of St. Doulough, near Dublin, is furniſhed with a fire-place, a fact which clearly demonſtrates that they were applied to the purpoſe of a habitation. Of the three doorways of Connor's chapel, two are very rich in ſculpture, and ſhow remains of the ancient Iriſh ſtyle, having a ſquare lintel, and upon that a ſemi-circular arch highly decorated.

The Round Tower on the north of the cathedral is a perfect one, and diſplays moſt of the peculiarities of theſe moſt intereſting remains of Iriſh antiquity. As the reader is aware, for a very long time there was much ſpeculation in Ireland amongſt the learned, and many theories regarding their origin. They were Daniſh, Phœnician, and half a dozen other things.

ROUND TOWER; ROCK OF CASHEL.

Their tall pointed character fuggefted that they belonged to the worfhippers of the fun and of fire. For a confiderable period this theory of General Vallancy and his difciples prevailed; but Dr. Petrie in his " Ecclefiaftical Architecture of Ireland," publifhed in 1845, put all thefe fancies to flight, and added a new intereft to them by clearly demonftrating that they were the work of the ancient Chriftians of the country; that they had been erected at different periods betwixt the fifth and thirteenth centuries, and had ferved for belfries, and for places of ftrength in cafes of attack by marauding enemies; as well as for watch-towers, from whence the approach of danger might be defcried. He imagines that they might alfo have ufed them as beacons. Thefe deductions he drew not only from their peculiar conftruction, but from the ancient Celtic MSS. of the country.

How clear now appears their origin. Thefe fingular and gloomy-looking tall hollow cylinders, with their lantern tops for the moft part, with their fmall loopholes generally larger near the fummit, and their loweft entrance at many feet from the ground, which the ancient Chriftians, no doubt, reached by a ladder, probably of rope, and which they drew in after them, feem now perfectly intelligible. Tolerably fecure, from the ftrength of the building and its refiftance to fire, having no wood about it, the Chriftian inhabitants could carry in with them their few valuables, efpecially their hiftoric and facred MSS., and could repel any affailants from the entrance, by having, as was frequently the cafe, another doorway above it, whence they could fling down huge ftones on their heads. This origin accounts fully for their always being in connexion with the old churches, or on the fpots where they had ftood, and on which more modern ones have been erected. The character of their doorways is fimilar to thofe of the primitive churches, narrowing upwards, fometimes with the fimple lintel, fometimes with a round and fomewhat ornamented arch. Over the main door they had frequently a crofs, or the figure of the crucifixion, in a ftyle allied to that of the churches. The round towers which I have feen were chiefly in the middle part of Ireland. A fine one, but much out of the perpendicular, ftands in the cathedral yard of

Kilkenny. I observed another on my way from Edgeworth Town to Auburn; and Dr Petrie particularly mentions those of Antrim; those at Donoughmore, in the county of Meath; at Timahoe and Kildare; at Clondalkin, Swords, Rusk and Rathmichael, near Dublin; at Monasterboice, near Drogheda; at Cloyne, in the county of Cork, and others. This round tower at Cashel indicates that the rock was the site of more ancient ecclesiastical erections than the present ruined cathedral.

Besides these sacred buildings on the rock, Cashel possessed several monasteries of much note. There was the old Dominican Friary, which was close to the site of the old Roman Catholic chapel. This was founded in the year 1243, by Archbishop Michael M'Kelly, who brought brethren from the Dominican abbey at Cork. It was destroyed by fire, and rebuilt in 1480, by John Cantwell, the archbishop, who promised to all persons aiding in its restoration the benefit of the masses, prayers, sermons, vigils, and other good deeds of the Dominican brotherhood throughout the kingdom during this life, and afterwards eternal happiness. A very liberal promise, if the recipients could have been assured of more infrangibility than promises are proverbial for. This friary is said to have been the noblest and most beautiful building belonging to the Dominican order in Ireland. At the suppression it was granted by Henry VIII. to Walter Fleming, of Cashel, for ever—tithes excepted—at an annual rent of 2s. 6d., Irish money. The ruins are now much decayed.

Then there was Hacket's, or the Franciscan abbey, on whose site the present Roman Catholic chapel was built. This was founded in the reign of Henry III., by William Hacket. In 1363 the abbey must have been in a very disorderly state; for a number of the friars by name were charged by the Lord Chief Justice, Sir Robert Preston, with cutting down timber, driving off the stock to the value of a hundred marks, and committing a variety of other enormities on his lands of Ballytarsyn and Le Hethon, for which offences he ordered the sheriffs to attach them. In 1538, the friars of the Strict Observance reformed this convent; but, if it had not been reformed before, it must have had about two centuries, or probably more, of disgraceful licenſe. At the diſſolution, Henry VIII. granted it for ever to Archbiſhop Butler, of Caſhel, at the annual rent of 2s. 10d., Iriſh money. In the night of the 14th of February, 1757, the lofty and beautiful ſteeple of this friary fell to the ground; and afterwards the ruins went rapidly to decay, till their outlines could ſcarcely be traced.

But the moſt important of all theſe monaſteries was Hore Abbey, or the White Friars. This was ſituated upon the plain immediately beſide the rock, and its fine remains continue in comparatively good preſervation. This abbey—called alſo St. Mary's Abbey of the Rock of Caſhel—was originally founded for Benedictines; but the archbiſhop, David M'Carvill, having dreamed, in the year 1269 or 1272, that theſe monks had made an attempt to cut off his head, he violently diſpoſſeſſed them, and gave their monaſtery to a body of Ciſtercian monks, whom he brought from the abbey of Mellifont, in the county of Louth, he himſelf at the ſame time aſſuming the habit of that order. The abbey poſſeſſed at this time much property, various extenſive lands, three mills, and a moiety of a mill, a church and a chapel; all of which were confirmed to the Ciſtercians by Edwards I. and II. At the diſſolution the catalogue of the abbey property was large. There were nearly twenty meſſuages, with their gardens and fields, amounting to nearly five hundred acres, beſides warren, tithes and alterages, a meaſure of ale out of every brewing in the town, called the Mary-gallon, with other privileges, and four churches. The bulk of this property was granted in 1561 by Queen Elizabeth to Sir Henry Radcliffe; but in 1576 it was re-granted on leafe to James Butler, and in the forty-fecond of the fame reign to Thomas Sinclair, at the annual rent of 2s. Irifh money.

In Archdall's time (1786) he defcribed the remains of Hore Abbey as in the following condition:—" The noble ruins of this erection ftill remain, and are, for the moft part, entire. The fteeple is large, and about twenty feet fquare on the infide, which is fupported by a variety of ogives from each angle, fome meeting in an octagon in the centre, and others at the key-ftones of the vault, and the ftructure is fupported by two fine arches, about thirty feet high. The choir, or chapel, which adjoins the eaft fide of the fteeple, is about twenty-nine feet in length, and twenty-four in breadth on the infide; the eaft window is fmall and plain, and in the fide walls are fome remains of ftalls, &c. The nave is fixty feet in length, twenty-three in breadth, and on each fide was an arcade of three Gothic arches, the north fide whereof is levelled, with lateral aifles, which were about thirteen feet broad. Between this and the fteeple is an apartment, but we are equally ignorant as to its name and the ufe to which it was applied. It is thirty-one feet in length, of the fame breadth as the nave, and divided from the fteeple by a plain wall. On each fide are fimilar arcades of two arches only, and this opens with the weft arch of the fteeple. On the fouth fide of the fteeple is a fmall door leading into an open part, about thirty feet long and twenty-four broad; the fide walls are much broken, and in the gable end is a long window. There is a fimilar divifion on the north fide of the fteeple. Here is a fmall arched apartment, which feems to have been a confeffionary, as there are niches in the walls, with holes, &c."

Such is the group of monafteries whofe ruins crown the

summit of the Rock of Cashel, or stand beneath its shade in the town, perhaps altogether the most remarkable in Ireland. They show that in the early ages of Irish history Cashel was a place of much importance. It was long the residence of the Kings of Munster, who had their palace on the rock; the ancient round tower probably being attached to the royal chapel. After 1101, the rock became wholly occupied by the cathedral, and the other ecclesiastical buildings. When Strongbow and his followers, by adopting the quarrel of Dermond MacMurrogh, the King of Leinster, against Roderick O'Connor, King of Connaught, Tiernan O'Ruarc, lord of Breffny, and other Irish chieftains, had made himself master of all Ireland, except Ulster, and Henry II. hastened over, in 1171, to secure the possession of the island to himself, it was near Cashel, on the banks of the Suir, that he received the homage of the King of Thomond or Limerick, the Prince of Ossory, and the other chiefs of Munster. Here again, after having visited Dublin, and received the homage of most of the other Irish chieftains, except those of Ulster, Henry called together a general council of the clergy to regulate the affairs of the church. At this council the sovereignty of Henry was fully acknowledged by the clergy. Between that important period, however, and the landing of King William III., Cashel was doomed, like most other Irish towns, to suffer many a blow in the different rebellions against the English rule, and by the punishments inflicted for these rebellions. What the Catholic clergy had to endure from the so-called Protestant invaders, may be imagined from what Miller in his " Letters to a Prebendary" relates ; namely, that on O'Hurle, the Archbishop of Cashel, falling into the hands of Queen Elizabeth's Governor, Sir William Drury, in 1573, he was first tortured by immersing his legs in jack-boots, filled with quick-lime, water, &c., until they were burnt to the bone, in order to force him to take the oath of supremacy, and he was then, with other circumstances of barbarity, hanged on the gallows.

During the civil war in the reign of Charles I., Lord Inchiquin, who had been one of the king's most zealous partizans, revolted against him, and fell with fury on the Catholics. He had long commanded in Ireland, though without the title of Lord President; and when the Earl of Portland was named by Charles to that office, Inchiquin was so incensed, that he went over to the Parliament, and set himself diligently to work to prove his zeal in the cause of his new masters. He made his officers and soldiers take the covenant, and bound them by a solemn oath to effect the total extirpation of popery, and the subjugation of the Irish. He proceeded to seize Cork, Youghal, and Kinsale, and drove out all the Catholic inhabitants, and plundered them of their effects. But his crowning atrocity was that at Cashel. "There," says Leland, "the inhabitants fled to their cathedral, seated on a rock well fortified, and provided with a strong garrison. Inchiquin proposed to leave them unmolested, on condition that they paid him over £3,000, and a month's pay to his army. But, as this proposal was rashly rejected, he took the place by storm, with considerable slaughter, both of the citizens and soldiers. Here he gained a prodigious booty. In storming the rock of Cashel, about twenty ecclesiastics fell in the indiscriminate slaughter; an incident shocking to the nuncio, who inveighed against this sacrilege, and clamoured for revenge." Castlehaun says that he put to death three thousand people, including many gentry who had fled to the rock for safety, and took the priests from under the very altars.

"Inchiquin," says Taylor, "was the lineal descendant of the royal race of the O'Briens; but there never was a scourge

of Ireland animated by a greater hatred of his countrymen.
Whether fighting for the king or the parliament — and he
changed fides more than once—he was invariably the bitter
enemy of his countrymen, and the favage profaner of the

ROCK OF CASHEL: NORTH TRANSEPT OF CATHEDRAL.

religious edifices in which the afhes of his own anceftors
repofed. His name is preferved in the traditions of Munfter,
as the fymbol of everything that is wicked and terrible. Nurfes
fcare their children by the threat of calling *black Murrough
O'Bryan;* and the fuperftitious peafant tells of the curfe that
he brought upon his family; and the failure of male heirs to
the title of Inchiquin."

Holy-Crofs Abbey.

"RELAND," fays Harris in his preface to his edition of "Ware's Antiquities," "has been diftinguifhed among other nations by the title of the Ifland of the Saints, for the vigilance of its reformers from heathenifm, and the perfeverance of the nation in the practice of the ftricteft moral and religious duties." Arienus, many centuries ago, following ftill earlier writers, called it the holy ifland. We may, therefore, fuppofe that Ireland, from a very early period, abounded with monafteries and nunneries. One of the moft facred and efteemed of thefe eftablifhments was Holy-Crofs Abbey in Tipperary. It was founded for monks of the Ciftercian order, in honour of the Holy Crofs of St. Mary and St. Benedict. It ftood on the right bank of the Suir, about three miles from Thurles, and near it a village. It was named the Abbey of the Holy Crofs, from a fragment of the true crofs which Pope Pafcal II. fent to Murtough, King of Ireland, in 1110. The abbey, however, was not founded till 1182, by Donogh Carbragh O'Brien, King of Limerick. The founder conferred on it extenfive lands, and Gregory was its firft abbot. It received further endowments and privileges from Kings John, Henry III., Richard II., the Earls of Ormond, and the Archbifhop of Cafhel.

The abbey was a daughter of the Abbey of Nenagh, Magy,

or Maig, in the County of Limerick, which was alſo founded by O'Brien, and, itſelf a daughter of Mell, became the mother of many others. The abbot of Holy Croſs was a baron of Parliament, and ſtyled Earl of Holy Croſs. He was uſually the vicar-general of the Ciſtercian order in Ireland. Jungelin, in his time, ſaid that it was incredible what a number of Iriſh Catholics ſtill continued their reſort to this church on account of the piece of our Saviour's croſs kept there. In the winter of 1559, the great rebel O'Neill made a pilgrimage to the piece of the croſs, and this ſaid fragment is affirmed to be ſtill in the poſſeſſion of the Roman Catholics of the place.

The incident juſt thrown in by the topographer, of the great rebel, O'Neill, making a pilgrimage to the fragment of the croſs at Holy-Croſs Abbey, is juſt one of thoſe dry bones ſtripped of every particle of living fleſh, of which our topographies generally conſiſt. How little does the reader ſee of the real fact in this dry incidental ſtatement. It is only when he turns to hiſtory, and aſks who was this O'Neill, and what were the circumſtances under which he made this pilgrimage, that he finds himſelf in the midſt of ſcenes which tell a ſtartling tale of what Ireland and what England were at that day, the much-vaunted day of Queen Elizabeth. Around this picturesque pile of Holy-Croſs there combated the wild children of a wild land, for their ſoil and their religion, againſt the Raleighs, the Spenſers, and the Eſſexes of England. Then indeed did the oppreſſed native of Ireland cling to every ſymbol and abode of his faith with a half deſpairing, half deſperate energy, and ſaw that Proteſtantiſm,—which ſhould have been mild and merciful, becauſe it boaſted itſelf more enlightened,— libelled by greedy ſtateſmen, and even by the worſhippers of the muſes, who were graſping at the poſſeſſions of their neighbours, and reigning amid fire and bloodſhed over the deſolated lands of the Irish. The picture of those days, as they are limned by Samuel Smiles, author of the "Life of George Stephenson," in his History of Ireland, shows us what are the memories that to this day still rankle in the hearts of the children of Erin, and render them insensible to the better treatment of to-day. It may be well to quote a few passages from a writer so well known for his moderate and judicious spirit :—

"At the accession of Elizabeth, Ireland was in a state of distraction. In the north, O'Neill was struggling to make himself master of Ulster, in which he had nearly succeeded ; in Connaught, the rival branches of the De Burgh family were making fierce and destructive war on each other : Munster was again distracted by the feuds of the Butlers and the Geraldines, and by struggles for the chieftaincy of the province; while Leinster was overrun by the men whom the barbarous persecution of the English Government had made landless, homeless, and desperate.

"One of the first acts of the Earl of Essex, the Queen's Lord-deputy, was to convene a parliament, and pass the famous Acts of Supremacy and Conformity for the re-establishment of the Reformed religion. These Acts were levelled at the whole fabric of Catholicism in Ireland : they transferred the primacy from the Pope to the Queen, and vested in her and the English Parliament the spiritual power to decide in all errors and heresies in the Church. The work of Protestantizing the Irish then commenced in earnest. The priesthood, who refused to change their opinions at the command of the Queen, were driven at once from their cures, and their places supplied by the scum of the English Church—men whom the English poet Spenser describes as guilty of 'gross simony, greedy covetousness, fleshly incontinence, careless sloth, and generally all difordered life.' The new clergy, befides, were men who did not know a word of the language of the people among whom they were fent to minifter; they had no fympathy for them; but, on the other hand, were leagued with thofe whom the Irifh naturally looked upon as their malignant enemies and oppreffors. How different from the native Catholic clergy of Ireland!—men fprung from the people, devotedly attached to them, fympathizing with their forrows, fharing in their fufferings, and fparing no toil or labour in the performance of their religious duties. All the powers of the moft perfecuting government that ever exifted could have no influence upon the convictions of a people miniftered to by a priefthood fuch as this. And they had not. Elizabeth had tried all forms of perfecution with the Irifh, even to the length of extermination, and they failed. She and her armies might conquer the foil of Ireland; but they could not conquer the deeply-rooted religious convictions of its inhabitants. Long, indeed, before the conclufion of her reign, Proteftantifm had made itfelf thoroughly odious and intolerable to the great mafs of the Irifh people.

"The plan which the government of Elizabeth feems to have premeditatedly adopted, and rigidly adhered to during her reign, was that of coercion and fubjugation of the Irifh. At one period, nothing fhort of utter extermination was thought of. With this view, chieftains were incited to make war upon each other, the agents of the government watching the opportunity to pounce upon them, and divide their eftates amongft themfelves. When diftricts could not be goaded to rebellion, other excufes were always found ready at hand. An infamous act was never yet done by wicked men, but there was an excufe to prop it up with. Thus, when chiefs did not actually rebel, it was eafy to accufe them of *intending* to rebel; and the fame object was accomplished as if they had been taken in actual rebellion. The firſt chief with whom the new policy was tried, was the powerful John O'Neill of Ulſter. A large force was marched againſt him, which O'Neill prepared vigorouſly to refiſt. An accommodation, however, was effected between the Lord-deputy and the chief, and blood-ſhed was for a time averted. The chief ſeized the opportunity of proceeding to London with all ſpeed, to lay his caſe before Queen Elizabeth in perſon. His appearance at the Engliſh court, in the character, dreſs, and following of an Iriſh chief, cauſed a great ſenſation. The fight-loving Londoners were delighted with the novelty; and Elizabeth felt flattered by the deference of the 'wild Iriſh chief.' The reſult was that O'Neill gained his point; and returned to Ireland, confirmed in all his honours, and in the poſſeſſion of all his vaſt eſtates." Elizabeth, in fact, created him Earl of Tyrone; or Tir Owen, as the Engliſh called him.

Camden, ſpeaking of this Shane-Dymas, or John O'Neill, and his viſit to London, ſays:—" He had 600 men for his guard, 4,000 foot, 1,000 horſe for the field. He claimed ſuperiority over all the lords of Ulſter, and called himſelf king thereof. When commiſſioners were ſent to treat with him, he ſaid 'that, though the Queen were his Sovereign lady, he never made peace with her, *but at her lodging;* that ſhe had made a wife earl of Macartymore, but that he kept as good a man as he. That he cared not for ſo mean a title as earl; that his blood and power were better than the beſt; that his anceſtors were kings of Ulſter; and that he would give place to none.' His kinſman, the Earl of Kildare, having perſuaded him of the folly of contending with the crown of England, he reſolved to attend the Queen, but in a ſtyle ſuited to his princely dignity. He appeared in London with a magnificent train of Irish galloglasses, arrayed in the richest habiliments of their country, their heads bare, their hair flowing on their shoulders, with their long and open sleeves dyed with saffron. Thus dressed, and surcharged with military harness, and armed with battle-axes, they afforded an astonishing spectacle to the citizens, who regarded them as the intruders of some very distant part of the globe. But at court his versatility now prevailed; his title to the sovereignty of Tyrone was pleaded from English laws and Irish institutions; and his allegations were so specious, that the Queen dismissed him with presents and assurances of favour. In England this transaction was looked upon as the humiliation of a repenting rebel: in Tyrone it was considered as a treaty of peace between two potentates."

" The Queen's English agents in Ireland were enraged at being thus out-manœuvred by O'Neill. They continued to represent to the Queen the danger of allowing such a person to remain possessed of such vast powers, and constantly asserted that he was on the brink of insurrection. 'Well,' at length replied Elizabeth, ' if he do revolt, it will be the better for you, as *there will then be estates enough for you all.*' However Elizabeth may have meant this—and she was a woman heartless and selfish enough for anything—her Irish retainers construed it into a licence to provoke the native chiefs into revolt, that they might share amongst them the estates which might thus be forfeited. Certainly means were immediately thereafter adopted to provoke O'Neill to rebellion. His resistance to the Government was at first effectual; but only a short time elapsed before he was completely crushed by their overwhelming power, as well as by the defection of those on whom he had counted as allies. In his last extremity, he fled to the Hebridian Scots, whom he had formerly attacked and routed with great flaughter, to gain the favour of the Englifh queen. In revenge, and inftigated by Piers, a Britifh officer, they flew him, and his head was fent to Dublin, as a trophy of the victory."

Then follows the long and revolting ftory of the fharing up of O'Neill's vaft eftates amongft the Englifh officers and gentlemen, and the fame perfecution, purfuing to death, and carving up of the great eftates in Munfter of the Earl of Defmond, a defcendant of one of the Anglo-Norman barons, who firft invaded Ireland under Strongbow. " The ferocity and cruelty with which this war was conducted," fays Mr. Smiles, " is perhaps unfurpaffed in the records of crime. Slaughter, famine, and defolation, marked the route of the Englifh army. No quarter was given. Men, women, and children, wherever found, were indifcriminately put to death. Soldiers were mad for blood. Priefts were murdered at the altar, and children at their mother's breafts. The beauty of women, the venerablenefs of age, the innocence of youth, were no protection againft thefe fanguinary demons in human form. The foldiers in the camp,' fays Holinfhed, the Englifh chronicler, ' were fo hot upon the fpur, and fo eager upon the vile rebels, that they fpared neither man, woman, nor child, but *all* were committed to the fword.' Neither was their cruelty glutted with bloodfhed. According to Lombard, a contemporary writer, ' great companies of thefe provincials, men, women, and children, were often forced into caftles, and other houfes, which were then fet on fire.' All cattle were carried away by the invaders, and crops cut down in fheer wantonnefs. What they could not carry with them they deftroyed with the flames. Famine and defolation were their handmaids ; thofe who were not flain with the fword perifhed with hunger. ' They performed,' fays Cox, another old Englifh writer, ' their duty fo effectually, and brought the rebels to fo low a condition, that they faw three children eating the entrails of their dead mother, upon whofe flefh they had fed many days, and roafted it with a flow fire.' We take a poet's defcription of the hideous fcenes of defolation which Ireland prefented at this period. "Notwithftanding," fays Edmund Spenfer, 'that the fame was a moft rich and plentiful country, yet, in one year and a half they were brought to fuch wretchednefs, as that any ftrong heart would rue the fame. Out of every corner of the woods and glynns they came creeping forth upon their hands, for their legs could not bear them; they looked like anatomies of death; they fpoke like ghofts crying out of their graves; they did eat the dead carrions, happy when they could find them, yea, and one another foon after; infomuch that the very carcafes they fpared not to fcrape out of their graves; and if they found a plot of water-creffes or fhamrocks, there they flocked as to a feaft for the time, yet not able to continue withal; that in fhort fpace there was none almoft left, and a moft populous and plentiful country fuddenly left void of man and beaft.'

And though Spenfer fpeaks here rather pityingly of the poor Irifh, yet, in his "View of the State of Ireland," he recommended ftarving them down till "they would quietly confume themfelves and devour one another." Sir Walter Ralcigh is charged with maffacring in cold blood, and after furrender, a Spanifh garrifon at Smerwick, in Kerry,—maffacring them to a man; and for fuch deeds he received 40,000 acres of the eftate of the murdered Earl Defmond, and Spenfer received Kilcolman Caftle and property, which was in turn burnt over his head by the incenfed Irifh.

At length Queen Elizabeth was informed that "nothing was left in Ireland but carcafes and afhes:" and Sir George

Carrew, one of the actors in thefe horrid fcenes, wrote an account of thefe infernal proceedings in a book called " Hibernia Pacata,"—" Ireland Pacified !" It was fo completely " pacified " that Holinfhed fays, " The land itfelf, which before thefe wars was populous, well inhabited, and rich in all the bleffings of God, being plenteous of corn, full of cattle, well ftored with fruit, and fundry other good commodities—is now wafte and barren, yielding no fruits ; the paftures no cattle ; the fields no corn ; the air no birds ; the feas, though full of fifh, yet to them yielding nothing. Finally, every way, the curfe of God was fo great, and the land fo barren both of man and beaft, that whofoever did travel from the one end to the other of all Munfter, even from Waterford to the heart of Limerick, which is about fix-fcore miles, he fhould not meet any man, woman, or child, faving in towns or cities ; nor yet fee any beaft, but the very wolves, the foxes, and other like ravenous beafts."

Such were the fcenes which, in Queen Elizabeth's days, and through thofe of the Stuarts, furrounded thefe old monaftic halls, which we are accuftomed to regard as the haunts of peace and pious contemplation. The only wonder is that they efcaped the general ravage, and were fuffered to ftand at all. The only thing which protected even a fragment of thefe fine architectural walls, was the fact that they were become the property of the Earl of Ormond, granted by Elizabeth in the fifth year of her reign, with 160 acres of arable land, fixty of pafture and two of wood, in the town of Holy Crofs.

The great O'Neill, who made a pilgrimage to the fragment of the Holy Crofs, would no longer find it depofited in the Abbey of Holy-Crofs, but in fome Catholic church or chapel of the place. It was this O'Neill, or O'Neale, to whom Sir Walter Scott alludes in Rokeby :—

HOLY-CROSS ABBEY.

Who has not heard while Erin yet
Strove 'gainſt the Saxon's iron bit—
Who has not heard how brave O'Neale
In Engliſh blood imbrued his ſteel,
Againſt St. George's croſs blazed high
The banners of his Taniſtry,
To fiery Eſſex gave the foil,
And reigned a prince in Ulſter's foil?

Spenfer, the poet, defcribes the rude mode in which even chiefs like O'Neill occafionally lived :—" The wood is his houfe againft all weathers, and his mantle is his couch to fleep in. Therein he wrappeth himfelf round, and covereth himfelf ftrongly againft the gnats, which in that country doe more annoy the naked rebels while they keep the woods, and doe more fharply wound them, than all their enemies' fwords or fpears, which can feldom come nigh them." But Sir John Harrington tells us how this O'Neill lived at his camp, for he paid him a vifit at the time of his truce with Effex; and after noticing " his fern tables, and fern forms, fpread under the ftately canopy of heaven," he notices what conftitutes the real power of every monarch, the love, namely, and allegiance of his fubjects:—" His guard, for the moft part, were beardlefs boys, without fhirts, who in the froft wade as familiarly through rivers as water-fpaniels. With what charm fuch a mafter makes them love him, I know not; but if he bid them come, they come; if go, they do go; if he fay—do this, they do it." —*Nugæ Antiquæ*.

The Englifh, however, never ceafed to purfue thefe half wild but heroic O'Neills, till their followers were obliged to fay :—

> For Turlough's days of joy are done,
> And other lords have feized his land,
> And faint and feeble is his hand,
> And all the glory of Tyrone
> Is like a morning vapour flown.

This O'Neill was Hugh, the nephew of the former great Earl of Tyrone, who had fucceeded to his eftates, which had been reftored by Elizabeth once more, once more only to excite the cupidity of the Englifh fettlers. By thefe voracious harpies he had been, like his uncle, driven into rebellion, that his property might become forfeited. One general after another had been fent againft him only to be defeated. Sir John Norris, Lord Burgh, Sir Henry Bagnal, had all fucceffively been put to the rout; O'Neill was faft uniting the Irifh chiefs in a common refiftance to their oppreffors, and was feeking additional aid from Spain. Elizabeth, now trembling for her Irifh dominions, fent over her favourite, the Earl of Effex, to quell him. Effex was not more fuccefsful againft O'Neill than his predeceffors, and was glad to make a truce with him; which fo enraged Elizabeth that, to calm down her anger, he haftened to England, leaving Lord Mountjoy to manage affairs in his abfence.

It was during this winter of 1559, whilft Effex in London was vainly endeavouring to regain the favour of Elizabeth, and whilft Mountjoy was as vainly endeavouring to draw O'Neill into an engagement, that he paid his vifit to the piece of the true crofs. Perhaps it might be in hope to draw fome confolation from fo facred a relic, for the days were now very dark with him. Effex, who had dealt gently with him, was gone, and had himfelf fallen amongft courtiers who ftimulated his fovereign, and fuccefsfully, to fend him to the block. But he had left his kinfman Blount, Lord Mountjoy, and other able generals, who were preffing him hard, and never ceafed to prefs him till they had brought him to a humiliating peace. It was time! Such was the condition of his people, that Morrifon, in his "Hiftory of Ireland," fays,—" Some old women about Newry ufed to make a fire in the fields, and divers little children, driving out the cattle in the cold mornings, and coming thither to warm themfelves, were by thefe women furprifed, killed, and eaten; which was at length difcovered by a great girl breaking from them by the ftrength of her body; and Captain Trevor fending out foldiers to know the truth, they found the children's fculls and bones, and apprehended the old women, who were executed for the fact." Numbers of poor people, Morrifon adds, were found dead in the ditches, with the remains of nettles, docks, and other weeds in their mouths. Such were the refults of the fo-called endeavours to plant Proteftantifm in Ireland by "good Queen Befs."

From its prefent remains, Holy-Crofs evidences for itfelf that it was one of the fineft fpecimens of the pointed ftyle of architecture in Ireland. Archdall, in the "Monafticum Hibernicum," in 1786, reprefents the condition of the building as follows:—It confifts of a high fteeple, nearly fquare, fupported on each fide by a beautiful Gothic arch, and in the centre by a great variety of ogives paffing diagonally from each angle. On the eaft fide thereof there is a fmall chapel, twenty-one feet in breadth, and twenty-four in length. The roof is arched, and beautifully fupported by a number of ogives from the fides and angles. On the fouth fide is a Gothic tomb, which, according to O'Halloran, is that of the founder, with a crofs thereon, but no infcription. The tradition of the place, however, informs us that this tomb was erected for the good woman who brought the holy relic hither. Between the nave and the fteeple is a fpace of twenty-one feet fix inches in breadth, and thirty in length, detached from the nave by an arch, which, we fuppofe, made a part of the choir. The nave was forty-nine feet broad, and fifty-eight long : on each fide is an arcade of four arches, with lateral aifles, which pafs on either fide of that part we conclude to have been the choir. The entrance is by a door at the weft-end, under a large window. On the fouth fide of the choir are two chapels, each about ten feet fquare, and both of them arched and fupported as the other parts of the building. Between thefe are a double row of Gothic arches, fupported by twifted pillars, each diftant about two feet four inches from each other: here the ceremony of waking the monks was performed; and not where the holy relic was kept, as remarked by a refpectable writer, in a plate which by miftake is reverfed. On the north fide of the choir are two other chapels, each of them eleven feet long and eleven broad, with roofs fupported in like manner with the others; and between thefe and the oppofite lateral aifle, the whole is arched; but oppofite the fouth chapel there is an open fpace, with a large flight of ftairs leading to the fteeple, &c., in the north angle of which are ftairs which afcend to the top. The difference in the work of this monaftery is very extraordinary;—nothing could have been more highly finifhed than the fteeple and chapels, which are built of marble and limeftone; yet the nave, the aifles, and adjoining ruins, are miferably mean. On the fouth fide the ruins cover a confiderable fpace. The river Suir, which, before it reaches the fea, is fo amazingly extenfive, flows near the ruins of this monaftery in a fmall ftream. A parifh church, with a few wretched cabins, are the only remains of a once celebrated town."

It may be fuppofed that fince this account was written, the remains of Holy-Crofs have fuffered further and confiderable dilapidation; yet Frazer, in his "Handbook of Ireland," fays that the ruins are ftill extenfive and picturefque, containing many interefting details, and amongft thefe is a tomb of Lady Eleanor Butler, fourth Countefs of Defmond.

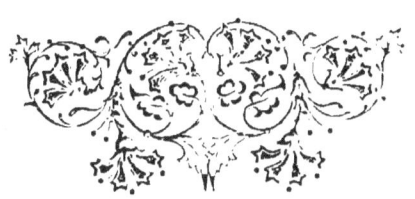

Cahir Caſtle.

AT about eight miles ſouth-weſt from Caſhel, and at the ſame diſtance weſt-north-weſt from Clonmel, and alſo on the Suir, ſtands the very pretty little town of Cahir. It has about 3,500 inhabitants, and, for its ſize, poſſeſſes the handſomeſt public buildings in Munſter. But it is ſtill more ſtriking from its very fine ſituation, and its ſurrounding ſcenery. The property of the town and caſtle is that of the earls of Glengall, who have preſerved the ruins of the caſtle from unneceſſary dilapidations, and have greatly improved the town generally. The ſituation of the caſtle is fine, ſtanding on an iſolated rock on the left bank of the Suir, and commanding views of the Galtee and Knockmealedown Mountains. Cahir is, in fact, ſituated at the foot of the eaſtern extremity of the Galtee range, and looking over the fine level lands ſouthward to the Knockmealedown range. At Cahir, the traveller finds himſelf in the centre of many natural beauties, and all of eaſy acceſs. The country round the town, the banks of the Suir, which runs through the town, and the finely-wooded park of the Earl of Glengall, are themſelves very attractive; but, beſides this, within eaſy drives are the mountains already mentioned, the Glen of Aharlo, and the caves of Mitchelstown. The Galtee Mountains are celebrated for their variety

of outline, their fertile slopes and picturesque glens; and the caves of Mitchelstown, about midway between Cahir and Mitchelstown, are near the south feet of these mountains. They have not been discovered many years, though they

CAHIR CASTLE.

are near the cavern of Skuhewinky, which has been long known.

It is asserted by modern archæologists that the builder of the present Castle of Cahir is unknown. Archdall and others attribute its erection to Conor-na-Catharach O'Brien, King of

Thomond prior to 1142. But it is contended that no caftle, properly fo called, of this clafs was erected in Ireland at that period, and that the fuppofition of Connor having built this caftle arifes from his having built a "cahir," or fort; but that this fort of his was not this on the Suir, but one on the ifland in Lough Derg, near Killaloe, which ftill retains his name. The ancient name of this town was originally *Cahir-duna-iafcaigh*, or the circular ftone fortrefs of the fifh-abounding dun, or fort; from an earthern dun, or fort, having ftood on the fite of a fubfequent cahir, or ftone fort, which was again fucceeded by a regular caftle. There is a record of the deftruction of the ftone fort as early as the third century, by the brother-in-law of Felemy Rechtmar, at which time it was the refidence of a lady of the name of Bodamar.

The prefent caftle was, no doubt, built by fome of the earlieft Anglo-Norman fettlers in Ireland. In the fourteenth century it was the refidence of James Galdie, or Butler, fon of James, the third earl of Ormond, by Catherine, daughter of Gerald, Earl of Defmond, whofe defcendant Thomas Butler, anceftor to the prefent Earl of Glengall, was advanced to the peerage in the 34th of Henry VIII., by the title of Baron of Cahir.

The chief hiftorical events connected with the caftle were the fieges of it by the Earl of Effex, in the reign of Queen Elizabeth, and by Lord Inchiquin, in that of Charles I. The readers of Englifh hiftory are familiar with the unhappy expedition of Effex to Ireland, which was greatly promoted by his powerful enemies at court, as certain to end unfortunately, and thus as certainly to break his influence with the Queen. Former viceroys and commanders in Ireland had fuffered difafter on difafter; and by the battle of the Blackwater, in 1598, the Englifh forces were reduced to the loweft ebb. Effex landed with an army of more than 20,000 men, the largeft force, according to the Four Mafters, fent to Ireland by the Englifh fince the invafion by Strongbow. But Effex was no more fuccefsful than his predeceffors. His orders were, in the firft place, to reduce the rebels in Ulfter, and to put ftrong garrifons into their forts; but, inftead of this, he marched into Munfter, and laid fiege to Cahir Caftle. He invefted it with 7,000 foot and 1,300 horfe; but the Earl of Defmond and Redmond Burk came to its relief, and Effex found himfelf unable to reduce it till he had fent to Waterford for heavy ordnance. On the tenth day of the fiege, being the 20th of May, 1599, the caftle was furrendered to the Earl of Effex and the Queen. But the furrender of the caftle was of no real advantage. He made, indeed, capture of the rebels' cattle in thofe parts, and drove the rebels themfelves into the woods and mountains; but, as faft as he retired again towards Dublin, thefe rebels came out from their retreats and followed on his track, haraffing his rear, fo that his return was rather like a rout than the march of a conqueror. The difafters which befell him on this journey completed his ruin; fo that the Four Mafters obferve :—" The Irifh afterwards were wont to fay that it were better for the Earl of Effex that he had not undertaken this expedition from Dublin to Hy-Conell Gaura, as he had to return back from his enterprife without receiving fubmiffion or refpect from the Geraldines, and without having achieved any exploit except the taking of Cahir-duna-iafgach." The Lord Cahir, Lord Roche, and fome others, made their fubmiffion; but this was only feigned, for they quickly rejoined the rebel party: and on the 23rd of May, in the following year, the Caftle of Cahir was furprifed and taken by the Lord Cahir's brother, as was fuppofed with his connivance. This furrender to the rebels, and its fubfequent recovery, are thus related by Sir George Carew, in his "Pacata Hibernia":—

"The President being at Youghall, in his journey to Cork, sent Sir John Dowdall, an ancient captain in Ireland, to Cahir Castle, as well to see the same provided of a sufficient ward out of Captain George Blount's company, as to take order for the furnishing of them with victual, municion, and other warlike provision. There he left, the 8th or 9th of May, a sergeant with nine-and-twenty soldiers, and all necessary provisions for two months; who, notwithstanding, upon the three-and-twentieth of the same, were surprised by James Galdie, alias Butler, brother to the Lord of Cahir, and, as it was suspected by many pregnant presumptions, not without the consent and working of the lord himself, which in after times proved to be true. The careless security of the warders, together with the treachery of an Irishman who was placed sentinel upon the top of the castle, were the causes of the surprise.

"James Galdie had no more in his company than sixty men; and, coming to the wall of the bawne of the castle undiscovered, by the help of ladders, and some masons that brake holes in some part of the wall where it was weak, got in and entered the hall before they were perceived. The serjeant, named Thomas Quayle, which had the charge of the castle, made some little resistance, and was wounded. Three of the wards were slaine; the rest, upon promise of their lives, rendered their arms, and were sent to Clonmell. Of this surprise the Lord President had notice when he was at Kilmallock; whereupon he sent directions for their imprisonment in Clonmell, until he might have leisure to try the delinquents by a marshall's-court. Upon the fourth day following, James Butler, who took the castle, wrote a large letter to the President, to excuse himself of his traitorly act, wherein there were not so many lines as lies, and written by the underhand working of the Lord of Cahir, his brother, they conceiving it to be the very next way to have the castle restored to the baron.

"Toward the latter end of the month of August, the Lord-Deputy, writing to the President about some other occasions, it pleased him to remember Cahir Castle, signifying that he much desired to have that castle recovered from the rebels; the rather because the great ordnance, or cannon, and a culverin being left there by the Earl of Essex, were now possessed by the rebels. This item from the Lord-Deputy spurred on the President, without further delay, to take order therein, and therefore, presently, by his letters, sent for the lord, who was vehemently suspected to have some hand both in the taking and keeping of it. The Baron of Cahir being come, the council persuaded him to deal with his brother, James Galdie, about the redelivery of it to Her Majesty; but his answer was, that he had no more interest with his brother than the meanest person had, for he was unwilling to have the castle regained by the state. The President perceiving this, let him know that if it were speedily yielded to him, he would entreat the Lord-Deputy to restore it to him; but, if not, he would march to the castle and rase it to the ground."

This had the desired effect. Lord Cahir, accompanied by Justice Comerford, rode away to the castle, and soon prevailed on James Galdie to surrender the castle to the Queen. Lord Cahir, notwithstanding his treachery, was pardoned by the Queen, and had his castle and estates restored to him in May, 1601, and died in possession of them in January, 1628; but his brother, James Galdie, lived to engage in the troubles of 1641, and suffered accordingly.

During this Lord Cahir's time, namely in 1626, Lord-Deputy Falkland was entertained by him with great splendour in the caftle, while on a tour through Ireland. On the death of this Lord Cahir, as already ftated, in 1628, the property was inherited by his only daughter Margaret, who married her kinfman, Edmund Butler, the fourth Lord Dumboyne, who, whilft refiding in this caftle with his wife, murdered in it James Prendergaft, the owner of Newcaftle. For this he was arrefted and confined in Dublin Caftle; but on his trial he was acquitted, fifteen of his peers voting him innocent, and only one, the celebrated Lord Dockwra, voting him guilty.

During the troubles following the rebellion of 1641, Cahir Caftle was invefted by Lord Inchiquin, who was then commanding for the Parliament. He carried its outer works, and compelled its furrender in a few hours. This was in Auguft, 1647, and again in February, 1650, Cromwell himfelf appeared before it, and his proceedings were very charaƈteriftic. They are thus related by Cliffe, the fecretary to General Ireton:—
"The place was poffeffed by one Captain Mathews, who was but a little before married to Lady Cahir, and had in it a confiderable number of men to defend it. The general drew his men before it, and, for the better terror in the bufinefs, brought fome cannon with him likewife, there being a great report of the ftrength of the place; and a ftory told the General that the Earl of Effex, in Queen Elizabeth's time, lay feven or eight weeks before it, and could not take it. He was, notwithftanding, then refolved to attempt the taking of it, and in order thereunto fent them this thundering meffage :

"'Sir, having brought the army and my cannon near this place, according to my ufual manner in fummoning places, I thought fit to offer you terms honourable for foldiers, that you may march away with your baggage, arms and colours, free from injuries or violence. But if I be, notwithftanding, necesfitated to bend my cannon upon you, *you muſt expect what is uſual in ſuch caſes.* To avoid blood, this is offered to you by

'Your fervant,

'O. CROMWELL.

'To the Governor at Cahir Caſtle,
  24th *February*, 1649 (1650.)'

"Notwithſtanding the ſtrength of the place, and the unfeaſonableneſs of the time of year, this ſummons ſtruck ſuch a terror into the garriſon, that the fame day the governor, Captain Mathews, immediately came to the General, and agreed for the ſurrender," etc.

This Captain Mathews, or Mathew, it appears, was the anceſtor of the celebrated Father Mathew, the apoſtle of temperance; an intereſting fact connected with the place.

In the "Pacata Hibernia" there is an accurate birds-eye view of Cahir Caſtle, as beſieged by the Earl of Eſſex; which ſhows that, notwithſtanding the lapſe of time, its great age, even at that period, and all the effects of ſtorms and winters ſince, it preſents very much the ſame appearance now as then, and from the care exerciſed for its preſervation by the preſent owner, it is likely to exhibit a ſimilar aſpect for ages to come. It ſtands on a conſiderable ſpace of ground, on an iſland, and has two bridges to connect it with the two banks of the Suir. It conſiſts of a great ſquare keep, ſurrounded by extenſive out-works, forming an outer and inner ballium, with a ſmall court-yard between the two; theſe outworks being flanked by ſeven towers, four of which are circular, and three of larger ſize, ſquare.

The view of the interior juſtifies the reputation for ſtrength which this caſtle poſſeſſed before the vaſt force acquired by cannon. Its ſtrong gateways, with their machicolations, their vaulted paſſages and portcullſſes, its vaulted dungeons and oubliettes, one of them having its roof covered with large flat stones, its trap-doors and gates of iron, imprefs you with a fenfe of the difficulty of affaillants breaking in, and of the impoffibility of unlucky prifoners breaking out. The Great Keep has a moft fingular oubliette or dungeon-hole made in the wall, very much like one of thofe in Germany, in which obnoxious prifoners were built up and left to perifh. The great hall has been reftored. The fummits of the building have been as carefully prepared for defence as any part below; and the whole prefents a very interefting fpecimen of fortification in the days when Whitworth and Armftrong guns were unknown. The marks of fhot are vifible all over the eaftern front of each building, in which direction it was attacked by Effex. Many of his cannon-balls have been found in the walls, and are now again replaced in the fpots out of which they had been taken. Many others ftruck, but did not penetrate, only chipping and fcaling away the outer ftone; the powder as well as the artillery of thofe days being far inferior to what they are now.

Richard Barrett, Printer, 13, Mark Lane, London.

www.ingramcontent.com/pod-product-compliance
Lightning Source LLC
Chambersburg PA
CBHW021825230426
43669CB00008B/865